The REXX Language on TSO

By Gabriel F. Gargiulo

Copyright 2015 Gabriel F. Gargiulo

Table of Contents

Introduction	**8**
Chapter 1: Overview of REXX	**11**
REXX features	**12**
Different ways to execute a REXX program	**13**
Example of a REXX Program, with explanations	**14**
Chapter 2: Setting Up to Execute REXX in TSO/ISPF	**17**
1. Create a PDS	**18**
2. Specify details for allocating PDS	**19**
3. Create a member	**19**
4. Create the SETUP member in ISPF Editor	**20**
5. Execute the Setup Program	**21**
6. Try it	**22**
Chapter 3: The Basic Features	**23**
The initial comment	**24**
SAY – display on the terminal	**25**
Variables	**26**
Reserved variables	**28**
The Literal	**30**
The Label	**32**
PULL – accept input from the terminal	**33**
DO for looping	**34**
Concatenating Data Strings	**35**
EXIT to end your program	**36**
Passing commands to TSO	**37**
Short Description of all of REXX's Verbs or Keywords	**38**
Chapter 4: IF	**41**
The simplest form of the IF	**42**
A few things to think about	**44**
Comparison operators	**45**
The DO END sequence	**48**
Boolean operators	**50**

Table of Contents

Chapter 5: Looping — **51**
The simplest form — **52**
The simple DO...END sequence — **53**
The DO number ... END sequence — **53**
The DO variable ... END sequence — **53**
The DO that increments a variable — **54**
The DO WHILE — **55**
The DO UNTIL — **55**
The DO FOREVER — **56**
LEAVE — **57**
ITERATE: Skipping back to the top of the loop — **58**

Chapter 6: SELECT: the CASE Structure — **59**
Example — **60**
Points of syntax — **60**
Several instructions: example — **61**

Chapter 7: PARSE — **63**
The basic form of PARSE — **64**
Origins — **65**
The Action of PARSE — **68**
Short forms of PARSE — **68**
Uses of PARSE: ARG — **69**
The ARG in a main program — **70**
The ARG in a user-written function or subroutine — **72**
Uses of PARSE: PULL — **73**
Uses of PARSE: EXTERNAL — **74**
Uses of PARSE: VAR — **75**
Uses of PARSE: VALUE — **76**
Uses of PARSE: SOURCE — **77**
Uses of PARSE: VERSION — **79**
PARSE Templates: Just Variables — **80**
PARSE Templates: A Literal — **83**
PARSE Templates: A Variable in place of a Literal — **85**
PARSE Templates: Column Delimiting With Numbers — **86**

Table of Contents

Chapter 8: Debugging — 89
- Interactive Debug — 90
  - What you can do during Interactive Debug — 90
  - Turning on Interactive Debug — 91
  - Codes displayed during Interactive Debug — 92
- Tracing: the Smaller Guns — 93
- Combinations of the TRACE verb — 94

Chapter 9: Trapping Unexpected Conditions — 95
- Situations you might want to trap — 96
- Trapping Unexpected Conditions: General — 97
- The trap that terminates — 97
- The trap that continues — 97
- Changing the name of the trap — 98
- Trapping Unexpected Conditions: Syntax — 99
- Trapping Unexpected Conditions: Error — 100
- Trapping Unexpected Conditions: Failure — 102
- Trapping Unexpected Conditions: Novalue — 103
- Trapping Unexpected Conditions: Halt — 104
- Trapping Unexpected Conditions: Contents of the Trap — 105

Chapter 10: SIGNAL: the Extinct "GO TO" — 107
- Signal: go there (but don't come back) — 108

Chapter 11: Math — 111
- When does REXX do math? — 112
- Math: Arithmetic Operators — 113
- Math: Precision — 114

Chapter 12: Passing Commands to Command Processors — 115
- Passing commands to the environment — 116
- How Do You Get REXX to Pass a Command to a Command Processor? — 117
- What Do the Return Codes (RC) mean? — 118
- What Command Processors Are Out There? — 120
- How do You Send Commands to a Command Processor? — 121
  - Sending commands to TSO — 121
  - Sending commands to ISPF — 122
  - Sending commands to the ISPF Editor — 124
- How Does Your Program Know if the Command Processor is There? — 126

Table of Contents

Chapter 13: Built-in Functions — **127**
Some examples — 128
Basics of functions — 128
CALLing a function — 129
Some of the more important functions. — 130
Those Conversion Functions — 132
Built-in Functions: TSO Functions — 134

Chapter 14: Writing Your Own Functions — **139**
Example of Internal Function — 140
Internal, user-written functions — 140
What makes a function a function? — 142
Protecting Variables — 143
Example of External Function — 144
External, user-written functions — 144
Search Order for Functions and Subroutines — 145

Chapter 15: Writing Your Own Subroutines — **147**
Example — 148
Writing internal subroutines — 148

Chapter 16: The Internal Data Queue, or Stack — **149**
What is it? — 150
How do you put things into the Internal Data Queue — 150
Internal Data Queue or terminal dialogue? — 151
Functions used with the Internal Data Queue — 152
Leftovers — 153
Clean up after yourself — 153

Chapter 17: Compound Variables — **155**
Compared to traditional subscripted variables — 156
Understanding Compound Variables — 157
Examples — 158

Table of Contents

Chapter 18: Reading and Writing Files: EXECIO — 161
The Basics — 162
The ALLOCATE command for reading — 163
Reading with EXECIO — 164
Reading whole file with EXECIO into Internal Data Queue – example — 165
Reading one record at a time into Internal Data Queue – example — 166
Reading whole file with EXECIO into an array – example — 167
Additional options for Reading — 168
The ALLOCATE command for writing — 169
Writing with EXECIO — 170
Writing whole file from Internal Data Queue – example — 171
Writing whole file from an array – example — 172

Chapter 19: The INTERPRET Instruction — 175
Why INTERPRET? — 176

Chapter 20: Running REXX in Batch — 179
Example — 180

Chapter 21: Example Programs, with Explanations — 181
STQUICK Program — 182
CANJOB Program — 184
SUBJCL1 Program — 186
SUBJCL2 Program — 188
SUBJCL3 Program — 192
UPDTMEMB Program — 196
CONTAINS Function — 200
EQWILD Function — 202
$HIDEALL Macro — 204

Index — 207

Introduction

Welcome to the REXX programming language.

REXX is an interpreted language used in several environments, such as:
- z/OS, (formerly called MVS and OS390) operating system
- JCL Batch jobs running under z/OS
- Netview for automated operations under z/OS
- z/OS TSO/ISPF Services for Panel Display
- QMF (Query Management Facility, a means for executing SQL)
- VM/CMS operating system
- CICS on-line system
- DOS/VSE operating system
- AIX
- AS400
- Linux

This book is about REXX under MVS/z/OS TSO. If you are interested in REXX as it is found in another environment, you can use this book to learn REXX anyway. There are minor language differences with REXX in different environments. The only features of REXX where you'll see significant differences are in the environment-specific functions and in the way you read and write files. Throughout the text I'll tell you when a feature of REXX works that way only on TSO.

REXX is a high level procedural language. It is on the same level as procedural languages such as COBOL, FORTRAN, PLI, Basic and C in which you solve the problem at hand step by step, figuring out the right order in which to do things.
It is a complete programming language and includes facilities for reading and writing files, although it is limited to the simplest file structure.

Introduction

REXX gets its strength from its powerful string manipulation verb PARSE, the simplicity of its logic structures and its numerous built-in functions that take the place of complex instructions.

It is often used to execute operating system commands under the control of its logic. Because of this it is known as a Command Procedure Language. To get more out of REXX you need to know operating system commands. If you are using REXX under z/OS you should know TSO commands. If you don't, you can get my paper through the internet at: http://TheAmericanProgrammer.com/programming/tsocmd.shtml and in my book on REXX functions, described just below.

It is generally used without compilation, so this limits its execution speed; however this will be offset by the speed of development and the power of its instructions.

The REXX you'll be seeing in this book isn't object-oriented; however NETREXX is and promises to do what Java does without turning your brain to ground beans. If you learn REXX you'll have no problem learning NETREXX.

The Internet Connection
Rather than make this a 300 page book, I've made much more information available through the Internet and in another book.

For the REXX functions and a tutorial on TSO commands, see my book: *The REXX Language on TSO: **REXX Functions**,* ISBN-10: 1490536078, ISBN-13: 978-1490536071, available for purchase at online booksellers and where you bought this book.

If you are converting CLIST programs to REXX, you will find this book useful: *TSO CLIST to TSO REXX: Conversion Handbook,* ISBN-10: 1508668493, ISBN-13: 978-1508668497, available for purchase at online booksellers and where you bought this book.

Further information on REXX: http://TheAmericanProgrammer.com/programming/rexxfiles.shtml

ISPF Edit macros. Paper at:
http://TheAmericanProgrammer.com/programming/holymac.shtml

REXX with the ISPF Dialogue Manager. The book is described here, but it is no longer available for purchase at: http://TheAmericanProgrammer.com/programming/dmbook.shtml

Introduction

Practice problems and suggested answers that go with this book. You can find them on my website and on the CBT tape.
http://TheAmericanProgrammer.com/programming/rexx2.prob.shtml
On the CBT Tape, here: http://www.cbttape.org/cbtdowns.htm
Scroll down to File # 911.

All the examples shown and explained in Chapter 21 of this book: you can find them on my website and on the CBT tape.
http://TheAmericanProgrammer.com/programming/rexx2.examples.shtml
On the CBT Tape, here: http://www.cbttape.org/cbtdowns.htm
Scroll down to File # 911.

Comparison of TSO/CLIST and REXX at:
http://TheAmericanProgrammer.com/programming/rexx.clist.shtml

More information about setting up to execute REXX on TSO at:
http://TheAmericanProgrammer.com/programming/rexxsetp.shtml

A very good description of TSO Line Mode commands, such as ALLOCATE:
http://TheAmericanProgrammer.com/programming/tsocmd.shtml

Links to a large number of on-line IBM manuals:
http://TheAmericanProgrammer.com/programming/manuals.shtml

An entire page listing published books on REXX programming:
http://TheAmericanProgrammer.com/books/books.rexx.shtml

REXX, TSO, ISPF, MVS, OS/390, VM/CMS, AS/400 z/OS, are registered trademarks of the IBM Corporation.

Revised May 9, 2015, 50

Chapter 1: Overview of REXX

Chapter 1 is a bird's eye view. This will give you an idea of what REXX is like.

Chapter 1 contains:
    REXX features   12
    Different ways to execute a REXX program   13
    Example of a REXX Program, with explanations   14

Chapter 1: Overview of REXX

REXX features

A REXX program can be as simple as this:
```
/* REXX */
Say "Hello World!"
```
This simple example will display Hello World! on the screen.

There is absolutely no datatyping in REXX: you don't have to define your variables. Variables are created as needed and are dynamically defined so they can hold numeric or character data of varying lengths.

REXX has all the features of a modern structured programming language. You'll find the following in REXX:

- the ability to do math with unlimited precision
- a full-featured loop structure
- a complete IF THEN ELSE structure
- nesting of logic structures
- a fully-implemented Case structure
- the ability to do subroutine calls with or without data encapsulation
- the ability to create and use functions
- an internal Data Queue
- arrays (Compound Variables) with numeric or character string "subscripts"
- the ability to read and write simple sequential files

REXX makes it easy to do complicated things, particularly in processing data files with fields in no particular column position with or without field delimiters.

You'll appreciate REXX's ability to execute operating system commands and to read and manipulate their output.

Power comes with a cost, and this is noticed in processing large-volume files.

Chapter 1: Overview of REXX

Different ways to execute a REXX program.

1. On any ISPF panel except option 6: (Setup required. See below).
    ```
    ==>   TSO Tryrexx or TSO %Tryrexx
    ```

2. In the ISPF Editor: (Setup required. See below)
```
 EDIT          userid.REXX.EXEC(Tryrexx) - 01.00
 Command ===> save;tso %Tryrexx          Scroll ===>
  ****** ********** Top of Data **************
 000001 /* REXX Tryrexx */
 000002 Say "My REXX program works"
```

"%" before the program's name shortens search time for your program.
It says: "it is a REXX exec or CLIST"

3. On ISPF member list
    EX next to member name

```
EDIT              userid.REXX.EXEC
Command ===>                                             Scroll ===>
         Name       Prompt      Size   Created   Changed
_____    $I·                   10    2013/10/18  2013/10/18 17:14:56  RE
EX_____  TRYREXX               15    2013/10/18  2013/10/18 18:36:28  RE
```

4. ISPF option 6
```
                                ISPF Command Shell
    Enter TSO or Workstation commands below:
        ==>    Tryrexx or %Tryrexx  (Setup required. See below).
        ==>    EXEC 'userid.REXX.EXEC(TRYREXX)' EXEC /*(No setup req'd)*/
```

5. REXX in batch, with JCL, see Chapter 20.

6. Inside a REXX program
```
/* REXX
THIS WILL EXECUTE ANOTHER REXX PROGRAM 3 ways
*/
"TRYREXX"     /*(Setup required. See below)*/
"%TRYREXX"    /*(Setup required. See below)*/
"EXEC 'userid.REXX.EXEC(TRYREXX)' EXEC"
```

7. Inside a CLIST
```
/* THIS WILL EXECUTE A REXX PROGRAM   3 ways
TRYREXX   /*(Setup required. See below)*/
%TRYREXX  /*(Setup required. See below)*/
EXEC 'userid.REXX.EXEC(TRYREXX)' EXEC
```

8. In Native Mode TSO ("ready mode", or "line mode"). You type its member name.
```
Myclist or %Myclist /* (Setup required. See below). */
"EXEC 'userid.REXX.EXEC(TRYREXX)' EXEC"     /*(No setup req'd)*/
```

Chapter 1: Overview of REXX

Example of a REXX Program, with explanations

A picture is worth 1K words. Here is a sample program in REXX that doesn't do anything interesting, but illustrates REXX syntax.

Always start a REXX program with a comment.   In column 1, first line.
   Include the word REXX on the first line. Anything else is optional.
   Comment may be on one or more lines.
```
/* REXX
     illustrates REXX features
*/

/*Upper and lower case are equivalent
in REXX instructions and variables*/
say "HI"
SAY "HI"

/*Comment may be on same line as instruction*/
Say "HI"     /* Displays HI */

   /*No column rules for REXX*/
       My_Name = "MOE" /* Assigning value to variable*/
Say My_Name

/*A variable may be made numeric simply by giving it a numeric value.
   (No datatype declarations)
   You may do math on numeric variables.*/
Phone = 8002345678
Say Phone
Phone = Phone + 1
```

Chapter 1: Overview of REXX

```rexx
/*A command in quotes is sent to the host system.
  (TSO, ISPF, the Editor)*/
         "LISTCAT"

/*       A blank line does nothing              */

/*Case is significant in literals. (Literal in quotes!)*/
         SAY "HELLO"
         SAY "hello"

/*Semicolon optional at end of instruction.*/
         SAY "hello";

/*Semicolon is needed to put two instructions on same line.*/
         SAY "GOODBYE";SAY "HELLO AGAIN"

/*A literal should have quotes. If you don't use quotes,
  it is taken as a variable.
  If the variable has no value,
  it is taken as a literal and uppercased
  If the variable has a value, that is displayed. */
SAY HI     /* HI */
SAY hi     /* HI */

/*Assigning a value to a variable*/
Hi = "HI THERE!"
Say Hi     /* HI THERE! */
```

Chapter 1: Overview of REXX

```
/*Comma is used to continue an instruction to another line*/
SAY "HI",
        "THERE"


/*Function invocation has no space before the parenthesis.
Some functions require empty parentheses. Others have a parameter*/
Say Date()
Say Date("W")

/*CALL implies that you will RETURN*/
Call Mysub

/*EXIT ends the program.
   Optional if it would be last word in program.
    (note - RETURN ends an internal function or subroutine)*/
EXIT

/*The internal function or subroutine label has a colon*/
Mysub:

   Say "This is in the subroutine"

RETURN /*goes back to the instruction after the CALL*/
```

Chapter 2: Setting Up to Execute REXX in TSO/ISPF

Chapter 2 is about things you have to do before you run a REXX program for the first time using your TSO user id. This is how to run REXX in the online TSO/ISPF testing environment.
To run REXX in production, you'll need information from your technical support group.

Chapter 2 contains:
    1. Create a PDS   18
    2. Specify details for allocating PDS   19
    3. Create a member   19
    4. Create the SETUP member in edit   20
    5. Execute the Setup Program   21
    6 Try it   22

Chapter 2: Setting Up to Execute REXX in TSO/ISPF

Please follow the detailed steps shown on this and the following pages to set up for the first time you use REXX on TSO.
Steps 1 – 4 have to be done only once for each TSO user-id. Step 5 is done every time you log on to TSO, or split the ISPF screen. (The setup applies only to the half of the screen on which it was done.)

1. Create a PDS

Create a library or PDS using ISPF option 3.2.
Name: Its name should end in the type qualifier EXEC,
               although this is not a requirement.
               Example: 'userid.REXX.EXEC'

Attributes: The PDS may be defined as 20 tracks primary,
               20 secondary, 30 directory blocks.
               Record format FB, Record length 80. Block size 27920.
               unless your company uses something else.

TSO ISPF Option 3.2

```
Menu   RefList   Utilities   Help

                         Data Set Utility
 Option ===> A

    A Allocate new data set            C Catalog data set
    R Rename entire data set           U Uncatalog data set
    D Delete entire data set           S Short data set info
blank Data set information             V VSAM Utilities

 ISPF Library:
    Project   . .
    Group  . . .
    Type . . . .

 Other Partitioned, Sequential or VSAM Data Set:
    Data Set Name . . . 'userid.REXX.EXEC'
    Volume Serial . . .    (If not cataloged, required for option "C")

 Data Set Password . .     (If password protected)
```

PRESS ENTER

Chapter 2: Setting Up to Execute REXX in TSO/ISPF

2. Specify details for allocating library

```
Menu  RefList  Utilities  Help
Allocate New Data Set
 Command ===>
                                                                More:    +
 Data Set Name   . . . : userid.REXX.EXEC
Management class . . .                  (Blank for default mgmt class)
 Storage class  . . . .                 (Blank for default stor class)
  Device type . . . . .                 (Generic unit or device addrs)
 Data class . . . . . .                 (Blank for default data class)
  Space units . . . . . trk             (BLKS, TRKS, CYLS, KB, MB
                                         or RECORDS)
  Average record unit                   (M, K, or U)
  Primary quantity  . . 20              (In above units)
  Secondary quantity    20              (In above units)
  Directory blocks  . . 30              (Zero for sequential data set)
  Record format . . . . FB
  Record length . . . . 80
  Block size  . . . . .
  Data set name type  : PDS             (LIBRARY, HFS, PDS, or blank)
                                        (YY/MM/DD, YYYY/MM/DD
  Expiration date . . .                  YY.DDD, YYYY.DDD in Julian
```

PRESS ENTER

3. Create a member

Using the ISPF Editor create a member in your REXX PDS named SETUP.
First, go to ISPF 3.4, the dataset list.

```
DSLIST - Data Sets Matching userid.                Row 364 of 382
Cmd ==>                                            Scr ==> CSR
Command - Enter "/" to select action        Message           Volume
-----------------------------------------------------------------
         USERID.SAMPLE.DATASET.FILE.DATA    MIGRAT1
         USERID.SAMPLE.DATASET.FILE.EXEC    MIGRAT1
         userid.SAMPLE.DATASET.FILE.JCL     TST056
         userid.PROGRAMS.CLIST              TST171
  E /(SETUP)serid.REXX.EXEC                 TST078
         userid.SAMPLE1.CLIST               MIGRAT1
         userid.SAMPLE1.CNTL                MIGRAT1
         userid.SAMPLE1.EXEC                MIGRAT1
         userid.XREF.JOBS.PROCS.OLD         MIGRAT1
```

Type E /(setup) over the name of your PDS (Means edit this PDS, member SETUP). There is a space after E, but no space after /.

Chapter 2: Setting Up to Execute REXX in TSO/ISPF

4. Create the SETUP member in edit

First specify your profile preferences on the command line, Then type in the program.

```
EDIT          userid.REXX.EXEC(SETUP) - 01.00
Cmd ===> rec on;number off;caps on;nulls on all;hilite rexx     CSR
****** ******************** Top of Data ************************
==MSG> -Warning- The UNDO command is not available until you change
==MSG>           your edit profile using the command RECOVERY ON.
''''''
'''''' /* REXX SETUP */
''''''    TRACE C
'''''' "ALTLIB DEACTIVATE APPL(EXEC)"
'''''' "ALTLIB ACTIVATE   APPL(EXEC) DSN('userid.REXX.EXEC')"
''''''
''''''
''''''
''''''
''''''
''''''
''''''
''''''
****** **************** Bottom of Data ***********************
```

type in this short REXX program:
```
/* REXX SETUP */
TRACE C
"ALTLIB DEACTIVATE APPL(EXEC)"
"ALTLIB ACTIVATE   APPL(EXEC) DSN('userid.REXX.EXEC')"
```

Type SAVE on the command line, then PF3.
Press PF3 one or more times until you get to the ISPF Main Menu

The Editor Profile for REXX:	
Rec on	recovery on, in case of abend
Number off	REXX doesn't need line numbers
Caps on	convert all to capital letters, if you wish
Nulls on all	allows insertion of characters on the line
Hilite REXX	editor uses colors to show REXX syntax
Hilite logic	(optional) matches DO and END

Chapter 2: Setting Up to Execute REXX in TSO/ISPF

5. Execute the Setup Program

From the ISPF Main menu,
Type 3.4, then press ENTER
The Data Set List will appear.
Type M (Members) next to the name of your REXX EXEC PDS, as shown here:

```
DSLIST - Data Sets Matching userid.                Row 364 of 382
Cmd ==>                                            Scr ==> CSR
Command - Enter "/" to select action       Message     Volume
-------------------------------------------------------------------
           USERID.SAMPLE.DATASET.FILE.DATA
           USERID.SAMPLE.DATASET.FILE.EXEC
           userid.SAMPLE.DATASET.FILE.JCL
           userid.PROGRAMS.CLIST
    M      userid.REXX.EXEC
           userid.SAMPLE1.CLIST
           userid.SAMPLE1.CNTL
           userid.SAMPLE1.EXEC
           userid.XREF.JOBS.PROCS.OLD
```

The REXX EXEC library (PDS) member list appears:

```
DSLIST                userid.REXX.EXEC          Row 1 of 10
Command ===>                              Scroll ===>
            Name     Prompt   Size   Created    Changed
            REXX001           10     2013/10/18 2013/10/18
   EX       SETUP             15     2013/10/18 2013/10/18
            TEST001           10     2013/10/18 2013/10/18
```

Type EX (EXEC) next to the name of the Setup program.
Press ENTER to execute your Setup program

You can now use REXX programs, by specifying just the member name of the REXX program in the PDS. Executing the setup program needs to be done only once during a logon session, but if you log off or split the screen, you have to execute it again.

Of course, there are other ways to set up in order to execute REXX programs. Many of them are peculiar to a specific installation.

Chapter 2: Setting Up to Execute REXX in TSO/ISPF

6. Try it

Try a REXX program, to see if anything works.
Using the ISPF Editor (option 2) create a member in your REXX PDS
    name it, for example TESTREXX
    type in a short program in REXX,
    The following is an example:

```
/* REXX TESTREXX */
SAY "HELLO THIS IS A REXX PROGRAM"
```

    Type SAVE on the command line.
    Type TSO %TESTREXX on the command line.
    Your program should work.
    If three asterisks appear on the screen, press ENTER to clear them.

On Option 6, TSO Command Shell, drop the word TSO.

You can obtain more information about setting up to execute REXX on TSO at this Web address:
http://TheAmericanProgrammer.com/programming/rexxsetp.shtml

Using the Percent Sign
It is recommended that you put the percent sign before the program name when you execute your program. This shortens TSO's search time because it tells TSO that your program is either a CLIST or a REXX program and that TSO should search only in CLIST and REXX libraries.
Example:
    Type **TSO %TESTREXX** on the command line.

If your program ever goes into an unending loop, press the PA1 or ATTN key.

Chapter 3: The Basic Features

Chapter 3 is about the basics of REXX. Not everything, and not in great detail. Let's get started by looking at the most important components of REXX. If you had only a short time to learn REXX you would learn these things first.

Chapter 3 contains:

The initial comment	24
SAY – display on the terminal	25
Variables	26
Reserved variables	28
The Literal	30
The Label	32
PULL – accept input from the terminal	33
DO for looping	34
Concatenating Data Strings	35
EXIT to end your program	36
Passing commands to TSO	37
Short Description of all of REXX's Verbs or Keywords	38

Chapter 3: The Basic Features

The Initial Comment

Although it is not required in all environments and under all circumstances your REXX program should start with a REXX comment. If you do it this way, your program will work in all environments.

- Start it in column 1
- Start it on the first physical line of your program
- the minimum comment required is /* REXX */ with REXX on the first line
- other words are allowed inside the comment as well
- the ending delimiter, */, may be placed on a different line from the first.

Simplest example:
```
/* REXX */
SAY "HELLO"
```

Example with longer comment:
```
/* REXX program "TESTREXX" to illustrate
whether REXX works or not
*/
SAY "HELLO"
```

Chapter 3: The Basic Features

SAY – Display on the Terminal

REXX is simple. The way to display information on the terminal is with the SAY verb. Anything after the word SAY on the same line will be displayed.

Displaying a literal character string, or constant:
SAY "HELLO THERE"

Displaying the results of arithmetic:
SAY 1 + 1

> More on Math in Chapter 11

REXX will gladly do arithmetic on the SAY. Just don't put the arithmetic operators in quotes!

Displaying variables: (The next section will describe variables.)
NAME = "SUE"
SAY NAME

> Syntax Reminder:
> Separate words in REXX with spaces as you would in English.

Displaying the results of functions:
Say Date()

Displaying any combination of the above
NAME = "SUE"
SAY NAME "Today is" Date()

> Point of Syntax covered fully in Chapter 13
> the name of a function butts up against its open-parenthesis with no space.

Do Practice Problem 1.
Get the practice problems and their answers here:
`http://TheAmericanProgrammer.com/programming/rexx2.prob.shtml`
You will also find them on the CBT Tape, here: http://www.cbttape.org/cbtdowns.htm
Scroll down to File # 911.

Chapter 3: The Basic Features

Variables

REXX makes using variables easy. There is no variable declaration or definition. So there is no datatyping: all REXX variables may contain all types of data. The data may be of almost any length, with the limit being very large and installation-dependent.

You first use a variable by assigning it a value.

Assigning a literal value:
NAME = "SUE"

Assigning another variable:
FIRST_NAME = NAME

Assigning the value of a function
TODAYS_DATE = DATE()

Doing arithmetic:
TOTAL = 1 + 1

> It's great not to have to worry about datatypes,
> but watch out that you don't get the dreaded REXX error 41:
> `Bad arithmetic conversion`
> By doing arithmetic on non-numeric data.

With PARSE or its variations
  PARSE UPPER ARG NAME ADDRESS

Reading files (See Chapter 18)
  "EXECIO * DISKR INFILE (STEM RECD.)"

Controlled DO loops (the variable at the left of the equal sign is given a value).
  DO I = 1 TO 10
   .....
  END

Some functions or subroutines
  CALL "LISTDSI" "ABC.DATA" /*TSO only*/
  /* sets the variable SYSLRECL and others*/

For REXX to see and interpret a variable, revealing what is contained in the variable, the variable must not be in quotations:
SAY NAME
 not
SAY "NAME"

Chapter 3: The Basic Features

Naming variables in REXX has few surprises.

- Variable names must begin with a letter and may be as long as 250 characters.
- The underscore character may be used for readability.
- The period is not used for readability, but is used to separate the parts of Compound Variables. (Covered in Chapter 17)
- upper or lower case may be used as desired
- case is not significant in variable names
- suggested that you avoid REXX keywords as variable names
  `EXIT = "HI"` will work, assigning the variable EXIT the value "HI",
  but will also give you a very unreadable program.

You don't define or declare a variable in REXX. The first time you use a variable it should be to assign it a value. What happens if you don't?
A variable that was never given a value is taken as a literal but converted to upper case.
   `SAY Hello /*DISPLAYS "HELLO"*/`

REXX doesn't consider that an error exception, but you can ask it to with the NOVALUE exception trap. (Covered in Chapter 9).

Chapter 3: The Basic Features

Reserved REXX Variables

REXX has three variables with a predefined meaning. Using these for anything but their original purpose will cause 10% of your brain cells to deteriorate...

RC is the numeric return code of any operating system or environment command.
```
"LISTCAT"
SAY RC
```
A zero means that there were no problems. A positive number indicates some problem.
A negative number tells of a serious problem.
REXX does not understand these codes.
The operating system command manual will explain them.

SIGL is the line number of the source program that sent control to a subroutine, internal function, or exception trap.
```
ERROR:
Say "Line #" SIGL "sent control to this subroutine"
```

RESULT is the character string or number returned by a function (built-in or user-written) when it is invoked with a CALL.
User-written functions must set this by placing a character string or number on their RETURN statement. Built-in functions do it automatically.
```
/* in the main part of your program*/
CALL Length "ABCDEF"
Say RESULT
```

> Built-in functions are covered in Chapter 13.
> User-written functions are covered in Chapter 14.

```
/* or*/
CALL My_function
Say RESULT
```

> Reminder - RESULT is set only after a CALL

```
EXIT

My_function:
/* does some processing */
RETURN /*character string or number goes here*/
```

Chapter 3: The Basic Features

Here are some suggestions about using variables:

- Use meaningful names: ACCOUNT_NUMBER rather than NUM.

- Use meaningfully different names where different data items are involved:
  `INPUT_ACCOUNT_NUMBER` and `HOLD_ACCOUNT_NUMBER`
  rather than `ACCT_NUM, ACCTNUMBER,` and `ACCOUNT`

- Don't use the same variable name for two different purposes.

- Use upper and lower case if you like that style.
  ```
  First_name
  Account_number
  ```

- Describe all variables at the beginning of your program.
  ```
  /* ACCOUNT_NUMBER is the client's account number */
  ```

- Do not use REXX keywords or reserved variables. Don't do:
  ```
  EXIT = "QUIT"
  SAY = "HELLO"
  RESULT = 5 + 4
  RC = 4 + 5
  SIGL = 14 + 1
  ```

- Prefix "throwaway" variables with TEMP.
  ```
  TEMP_LENGTH = LENGTH("ABCDE")
  TEMP_LENGTH = TEMP_LENGTH / 2
  TEMP_LENGTH = ABS(TEMP_LENGTH)
  TEMP_LENGTH = 2
  SAY "TWO CHARACTERS STARTING AT THE MIDDLE ARE:"
  SAY SUBSTR("ABCDE",2,TEMP_LENGTH)
  ```

- You may undefine a variable and reclaim the memory that it is using with the DROP instruction.
  DROP NAME

Chapter 3: The Basic Features

The Literal

The literal is itself. It stands for nothing else. Literals are normally enclosed in double quotes or apostrophes.

```
"HELLO"
'GOODBYE'
12345
"12345"
HELLO
""/*this is the null string (zero characters)*/
"O'Connor"/*enclose an apostrophe in double quotes*/
'He said "Hello Ellen" when he saw her' /*enclose
         double quotes in apostrophes*/
1E+2 /* exponential notation. 1 to the 2nd power*/
"F1F2F3"x /* a hex string*/
```

If you forget the double quotes or apostrophes REXX will first look to see if the string of characters is a variable. If it is, then REXX uses the contents of the variable. If it isn't, then REXX takes the character string as a literal, but will convert it to upper case. I recommend you not make use of this feature.
```
SAY Hello /* Works, but not recommended*/
```

Continuing literals:
Although a literal may be up to 251 characters in length, you may not want to create a line that long. Instead, I suggest you concatenate two literals to produce a longer one. See the section Concatenating Data Strings later in this chapter.
```
LONG_VAR = "LONG STRING TO END OF LINE" || ,
           "REST OF STRING ON NEXT LINE"
SAY LONG_VAR
```
on the mainframe this character is the solid vertical bar (hex 4F)
everywhere else it is the broken vertical bar (hex 7C).

Some people like the following way to create a long literal that occupies more than one line. I do not like this way, but show it here for completeness.
```
LONG_VAR = "FIRST LINE, NO QUOTES AT END
  NEXT LINE, NO QUOTES AT BEGINNING"
SAY LONG_VAR
```

Chapter 3: The Basic Features

Some suggestions about using literals

- always use quotation marks or apostrophes around literals.
  ```
  SAY "HELLO"
  SAY 'HELLO'
  ```

- Don't use quotation marks or apostrophes around numbers. (although it will work)
  ```
  SAY "1" + "2"
  ```

- use quotation marks with TSO commands. Some TSO commands use apostrophes. This will avoid conflict.
  ```
  "SEND 'HELLO SUE' USER(TSOU01)"
  "DELETE 'TSOU02.JUNK.DATA'   "
  ```

- use apostrophes in environments other than TSO.
  ```
  'MSG * LUNCH TIME YET? '  /* a CMS command*/
  ```

Do Practice Problems 2, 3, 4.

Chapter 3: The Basic Features

The Label

A label is the target of a transfer of control instruction (**CALL** or **SIGNAL**).
It is used to name a subroutine, a user-written function, an exception trap or a place that you 'go to'.
(**SIGNAL**)
A label must be the first thing on the line and end with a colon.
The label may be alone on the line or there may be an instruction next to it.

Subroutines are covered in Chapter 15. Exception traps are covered in Chapter 9.

```
/* in the Main part of program:*/
     CALL COMPUTE
     CALL SUBROUTINE
     SIGNAL HERE
     SIGNAL ON ERROR

/*Near the physical end of the program:  */
     COMPUTE:   A = 1 + 3
     /* etc */

     SUBROUTINE1:
     /* instructions here */
     /* etc */

     HERE:
     /* instructions here */
     /* etc */

     ERROR:
     /* instructions here */
     /* etc */
```

Using Signal as a simple 'go to' is recommended only when it is to go to a routine that does some exception processing and terminates the program.
```
IF ERROR_COUNT > 100 THEN SIGNAL BAIL_OUT
/* intervening code*/

BAIL_OUT:
Say "Exception condition occurred"
EXIT
```

Chapter 3: The Basic Features

PULL – accept input from the terminal

Use PULL with a variable to read in something you type at the terminal.
You should place a SAY before the PULL so the user knows what to type in.
```
SAY "PLEASE TYPE IN YOUR NAME"
PULL NAME
```

PULL will convert to upper case.

When the program does a PULL it stops and waits for you to type something in and press ENTER.

PULL is actually more powerful than it appears to be here. PULL is a shorthand form of the PARSE instruction that is covered in Chapter 7.

PULL without a variable just stops the program and waits for you to press ENTER.
```
SAY "Press ENTER to continue"
PULL
```

Chapter 3: The Basic Features

DO for looping

DO allows you to repeat an instruction or several instructions. It can be used to initialize and increment a variable, and continue the loop until the variable reaches a certain value. This is equivalent to BASIC's FOR loop, COBOL's PERFORM, and most other languages' DO.

This example will initialize the variable INDEX to 1, increment it by 1 and continue looping until INDEX is greater than 10. While inside the loop it will display the variable INDEX.
Running this will produce the numbers 1 through 10.

```
DO INDEX = 1 TO 10
    SAY INDEX
END INDEX
```

There are many variations on this simple DO. They will be covered in Chapter 5.

C-hapter 3: The Basic Features

Concatenating Data Strings

This is about how REXX handles data strings that are placed next to each other on the line. There are three possibilities on how the strings can be separated:

- Separated by one or more spaces
    ```
    Say "Hi"      "Ellen"      /*displays Hi Ellen*/
    ```
    all the spaces are condensed to just 1 space.

- Strings abutting each other
    ```
    Name = "Ellen"
    Say "Hi"Name            /(*displays HiEllen*/
    ```
    no spaces are added.

- Strings separated physically but joined by the concatenation operator(||)
    on the mainframe this character is the solid vertical bar (hex 4F)
    everywhere else it is the broken vertical bar (hex 7C)
    ```
    Say "Hi" ||     "Ellen"     /*displays HiEllen*/
    ```
    any spaces present between the strings are deleted.

Do Practice Problem 5.

Chapter 3: The Basic Features

EXIT to End Your Program

The verb EXIT will end your program. It is not needed if it would be the last line in your program. It is needed if some other code, such as a subroutine, user-written function or exception trap follows the logical end of the program.

```
SAY "PLEASE TYPE IN YOUR NAME"
PULL NAME
SAY NAME
CALL Process_name_subroutine

EXIT

Process_name_subroutine:
/* do something to name*/
RETURN
```

You can put a number on the EXIT.
```
      EXIT 16
```
This will pass the number 16 to the program or command that executed your program.
If a REXX program executed your program, the number will be visible to the original executing program in RC.
If a CLIST executed your program, the number will be visible to the CLIST in **&LASTCC**.

If you don't put a number on the **EXIT**, a zero is used.

You may not put a non-numeric character string on the **EXIT**.
You may put a variable containing a number on the **EXIT**.
```
      RETURN_CODE = 16
      EXIT RETURN_CODE
```

Chapter 3: The Basic Features

Passing Commands to TSO

If you need to know more about TSO commands, see Supplement 1 in my book: *TSO CLIST to TSO REXX: Conversion Handbook,* ISBN-10: 1508668493, ISBN-13: 978-1508668497, available for purchase at online booksellers and where you bought this book.

To pass a TSO command to TSO, just place the TSO command first on the line, in quotations.

```
"LISTCAT"              /*sends a command to TSO*/
CMD = "LISTCAT"        /*doesn't send to TSO (assignment)*/
CMD                    /*sends contents of variable to TSO*/
```

Here is an example of a very simple TSO command: LISTCAT in REXX
It will display a list of catalogued files whose names begin with your TSO user-id.
```
/* REXX */
"LISTCAT"
```

The quote marks around LISTCAT are optional in this case due to its simplicity. However you will normally put your TSO commands inside of quote marks. This avoids having REXX try to interpret things it shouldn't be interpreting. The next example will illustrate:
```
/* REXX */
"SEND 'HELLO' USER(TSOUID2)"
```

It is passing the TSO command **SEND 'HELLO' USER(TSOUID2)** to TSO.
TSO understands this command; REXX doesn't. To keep REXX from trying to understand it you place it in quotations. Then REXX treats it as a literal and will not try to interpret it.

It gets a bit more interesting when you have a variable in the TSO command and you *do want* REXX to interpret the variable. In this case, leave the variable out of the quotations but keep the rest inside.
```
/* REXX */
USERID = "TSOUID2"
"SEND 'HELLO' USER("USERID")"
```
Although it is confusing to the eye, the variable USERID is outside of quotations and so REXX will see it and interpret it, changing it to its value (**TSOUID2**) and passing the entire line, as it sees it, to TSO.
It will pass **SEND 'HELLO' USER(TSOUID2)** to TSO.

Do Practice Problems 6 – 8.

Chapter 3: The Basic Features

Short Description of all of REXX's Verbs or Keywords

ADDRESS (Chapter 12)
    Passes commands to a specific environment or command processor.

ARG (Chapter 7) Receives information passed from the command line or function/subroutine invocation.

CALL (Chapters 9, 13, 15)
    Invokes a subroutine or function
    turns on or off an error trap that continues executing.

DO (Chapters 4, 5, 6) Begins a loop.

DROP (Chapter 3) Undefines a variable.

ELSE (Chapter 4) Introduces "false" outcome with IF.

END (Chapters 4, 5, 6) Terminates a DO loop.

EXIT (Chapter 3) Ends the program.

EXPOSE (Chapter 14) Allows sharing of a subroutine or function's variables.

IF (Chapter 4) Conditional execution.

INTERPRET (Chapter 19) Processes data as if it were an instruction.

ITERATE (Chapter 5) Goes to the beginning of a loop.

LEAVE (Chapter 5) Exits from a DO loop.

Chapter 3: The Basic Features

NOP does nothing.

NUMERIC controls precision, indefiniteness in comparisons, and exponential notation.

OTHERWISE (Chapter 6) Is the default alternative in the SELECT.

PARSE (Chapter 7) Is for string manipulation.

PROCEDURE (Chapter 14) Protects variables in a function/subroutine.

PULL (Chapters 3, 7) Removes data from the Internal Data Queue (Stack).
        Accepts terminal input.

PUSH (Chapter 16) Puts data into the Internal Data Queue (Stack), LIFO.

QUEUE (Chapter 16) Puts data into the Internal Data Queue (Stack), FIFO.

RETURN (Chapter 14) In a function/subroutine,
        sends control back to the instruction
        after the one that invoked the function/subroutine.

SAY (Chapter 3) Displays a line on the terminal.

SELECT (Chapter 6) Introduces the CASE structure.

SIGNAL (Chapter 10) Unconditional transfer of control.
        turns on or off a condition trap that terminates the program

THEN (Chapter 4) Introduces "true" outcome with IF.

TRACE (Chapter 8) Controls tracing and Interactive Debugging.

Do Practice Problems 9 – 19.

Chapter 4: IF

Chapter 4 is about REXX's full-function conditional verb: IF.
It is like IF in most languages, plus a few additional features.

Chapter 4 contains:
    The simplest form of the IF   42
    A few things to think about   44
    Comparison operators   45
    The DO END sequence   48
    Boolean operators   50

Chapter 4: IF

All programming languages have a conditional verb. REXX has a full-function IF.
It doesn't work exactly like IF in other languages. Here's what you should know about the REXX IF:

The simplest form of the IF:

```
IF comparison THEN verb-to-execute-if-true
```

comparison is:
- Variable operator variable
    IF A = B
- Variable operator literal
    IF A = 1
- Literal operator variable
    IF 1 = A
- Expression operator variable
    IF 1 + 1 = total (parens not required)
    IF (1 + 1) = total
- Expression operator literal
    IF (1 + 1) = 2

or some other combination of variables, literals, and expressions.
    IF 2 = (1 + 1)
    IF Name = "Sue"
    IF Length(Name) = 3
    IF Length(Name) = (2 + 1)
THEN is required

verb-to-execute-if-true
   may be any one REXX verb, instruction,
   assignment or operating system command.
   Note that there may be only one verb
       unless you use the DO...END construction. (Chapter 5)

   IF A = 1 THEN Say "It is true"

Chapter 4: IF

You may arrange words on the line in any one of these ways: (indenting as you desire)

```
IF comparison THEN verb-to-execute-if-true

IF comparison
THEN verb-to-execute-if-true

IF comparison THEN
    verb-to-execute-if-true
```

ELSE tells what to do if the condition is false
```
IF comparison THEN verb-to-execute-if-true
ELSE verb-to-execute-if-false
```

ELSE is not required
If you use it, ELSE must be on a new line
With ELSE you may arrange words on the line in any one of these ways:
    (indenting as you desire)

```
IF comparison THEN verb-to-execute-if-true
ELSE verb-to-execute-if-false

IF comparison
THEN verb-to-execute-if-true
ELSE verb-to-execute-if-false

IF comparison THEN
verb-to-execute-if-true
ELSE verb-to-execute-if-false

IF comparison THEN true-verb; ELSE false-verb
```

Chapter 4: IF

A few things to think about:

You may not omit variables as in COBOL. This is legal in COBOL, not REXX:
```
IF A = 1 | 2 ..../* no good */
```

Operators are shown in a few pages. English words such as EQUAL, AND, and OR are not allowed.

THEN is required.

THEN is followed by *one* instruction or by a DO ... END sequence

NOP may be used as a "do nothing" instruction.

ELSE is not required. It too is followed by *one* instruction or by a DO ... END sequence

Case is significant in comparisons. "Sue" is not equal to "SUE".

There is no 'END IF'. Its place is taken by the last END of a DO...END sequence after an IF. Be sure to comment this END so its use is obvious.

Nesting is allowed. Please write clear code with indenting and comments.

```
NAME = "SUE"
PAY = 100

IF PAY < 80000 THEN DO
    PAY = PAY * 1.2
    IF NAME = "SUE" THEN PAY = PAY * 1.5
    END /* PAY < 80000 */

    ELSE DO
     /* NO ACTION TAKEN */
    END /* PAY NOT < 80000*/
SAY PAY
```

Chapter 4: IF

Comparison operators

Note: ¬ has the hex configuration of 5F on the mainframe.
      | has the hex configuration of 4F on the mainframe.

Suggestion: avoid the characters that don't exist in all environments or keyboards or that file transfer utilities have trouble with: Avoid ¬ and ^ (hex B0).

You can't avoid |. Best approach is to check the character after doing a file transfer. Actually execute the code containing | to see if it works.

Use <> for 'not equal'.

The difference between = and ==

= Equal

= asks if two things are equal, accounting for leading/trailing spaces and numeric equivalency.

```
IF "JOE" = "JOE   "  THEN SAY "YES" /* are equal */
IF 100   = 0100.00   THEN SAY "YES" /* are equal */
```

== Strictly Equal

== asks if two things are exactly equal, on a character by character basis
```
IF "JOE" == "JOE   "  THEN SAY "YES" /*not equal*/
IF 100   == 0100.00   THEN SAY "YES" /*not equal*/

IF "JOE" == "JOE" THEN SAY "YES" /* are equal */
IF 100   == 100   THEN SAY "YES" /* are equal */
```

The same principle applies to ¬==, \==, >>, >>=, <<, <<=.

Chapter 4: IF

Comparison operators

= Equal. If numeric, when compared algebraically.
   (1.0 is equal to 001.000.)
   If not numeric, when padded with leading or trailing spaces.
   ("Sue" is equal to " Sue ".)
   Case is significant: "SUE" is not equal to "sue".

<> Not equal, the negation of "=".
    Algebraic comparison and padding are performed.

>< Not equal, the negation of "=".
    Algebraic comparison and padding are performed.

\= Not equal, the negation of "=".
    Algebraic comparison and padding are performed.

¬= Not equal, the negation of "=".
    (The symbol "¬" may not be found on all keyboards.)
    Algebraic comparison and padding are performed.

^= Not equal, the negation of "=".
    (The symbol "^" may not be found on all keyboards.)
    Algebraic comparison and padding are performed.

\> Greater than. Algebraic comparison and padding are performed.

<   Less than. Algebraic comparison and padding are performed.

>= Greater than or equal to. Algebraic comparison and padding are performed.

¬< Not less than. (The symbol "¬" may not be found on all keyboards.)
    Algebraic comparison and padding are performed.

\< Not less than. Algebraic comparison and padding are performed.

<= Less than or equal to. Algebraic comparison and padding are performed.

¬> Not greater than.
    (The symbol "¬" may not be found on all keyboards.)
    Algebraic comparison and padding are performed.

\> Not greater than. Algebraic comparison and padding are performed.

More ...

Chapter 4: IF

`==`	Strictly equal on a character-by-character basis. No algebraic comparison or padding is done.
`¬==`	Strictly not equal, the negation of "==". (The symbol "¬" may not be found on all keyboards.) No algebraic comparison or padding is done.
`\==`	Strictly not equal, the negation of "==". No algebraic comparison or padding is done.
`>>`	Strictly greater than. No algebraic comparison or padding is done.
`>>=`	Strictly greater than or equal to. No algebraic comparison or padding is done.
`<<`	Strictly less than. No algebraic comparison or padding is done.
`<<=`	Strictly less than or equal to. No algebraic comparison or padding is done.
`¬>>`	Strictly not greater than. (The symbol "¬" may not be found on all keyboards.) No algebraic comparison or padding is done.
`¬<<`	Strictly not less than. (The symbol "¬" may not be found on all keyboards.) No algebraic comparison or padding is done.
`&`	And. The conditions on both sides of this operator must be true.
`|`	Or. One or both of the conditions on either side of this operator must be true.
`&&`	Exclusive Or. Only one, but not both, of the conditions on either side of this operator must be true.

Chapter 4: IF

The DO END sequence

```
        IF A = 1 THEN do /* is equal */
           say "it is equal"
           say "really"
           end /* is equal*/
        ELSE do /* not equal */
           say "it is not equal"
           say "really, it's not"
           end /* not equal */
```

If you need more than 1 instruction after THEN, or ELSE use the DO...END sequence. There are several styles in common use.

Style 1
```
    IF A = 1 THEN do /* is equal */
       say "it is equal"
       say "really"
       end /* is equal*/
    ELSE do /* not equal */
       say "it is not equal"
       say "really, it's not"
       end /* not equal */
```

Style 2
```
    IF A = 1
    THEN do /* is equal */
       say "it is equal"
       say "really"
       end /* is equal*/
    ELSE do /* not equal */
       say "it is not equal"
       say "really, it's not"
       end /* not equal */
```

Chapter 4: IF

Style 3
```
      IF A = 1
      THEN
         do /* is equal */
            say "it is equal"
            say "really"
         end /* is equal*/
      ELSE
         do /* not equal */
            say "it is not equal"
            say "really, it's not"
         end /* not equal */
```

Style 4
```
      IF A = 1 THEN do /* is equal */
                  say "it is equal"
                  say "really"
                  end /* is equal*/
              ELSE do /* not equal */
                  say "it is not equal"
                  say "really, it's not"
                  end /* not equal */
```

A DO ... END with nothing between is valid.
```
      IF A = 1 THEN do /* is equal */
           end
      ELSE do /* not equal */
           say "it is not equal"
           say "really, it's not"
           end /* not equal */
```

Comments. Use comments on DO's and END's. This is especially useful when you have nested IF's with several DO's and END's.

Chapter 4: IF

Boolean operators

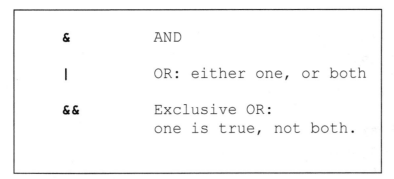

& (AND)
```
IF PAY_GRADE = 11 & NAME = "ELLEN"
THEN SALARY = SALARY * 2
```

| (OR)
```
IF PAY_GRADE = 11 | PAY_GRADE = 12
THEN SALARY = SALARY * 1.5
```

&& (Exclusive OR)
```
IF PAY_GRADE = 11 && EMPLOY_STATUS = "RETIRED"
THEN NOP
ELSE SAY "INPUT DATA ERROR"
```

The English words AND/OR don't work. They may not produce a syntax error but will produce the wrong results.
```
IF PAY_GRADE = 11 AND NAME = "ELLEN"
THEN SALARY = SALARY * 2
```
Will compare **PAY_GRADE** to the character string **11 AND NAME = "ELLEN"** and the results will be wrong.

Do Practice Problems 20 – 22.

Chapter 5: Looping

Chapter 5 is about REXX's repetition structure. All the code between a DO and an END is repeated, from 0 to N times.

A program that goes directly from top to bottom is a boring program. Most programs need to repeat their actions. Messy loops mean disastrous programs. REXX has neat loops.

Chapter 5 contains:

The simplest form	52
The simple DO...END sequence	53
The DO number ... END sequence	53
The DO variable ... END sequence	53
The DO that increments a variable	54
The DO WHILE	55
The DO UNTIL	55
The DO FOREVER	56
LEAVE	57
ITERATE: Skipping back to the top of the loop	58

Chapter 5: Looping

The simplest form

```
DO modifiers
/* instructions*/
END
```

Most programs will need to loop through a file or the elements of an array, or to continue some action as long as a condition is true.

REXX has a full-function loop: the DO ... END.
What makes REXX so powerful is that there are many variations on the simple loop: you can use the one best suited for your programming needs.

REXX offers these types of looping:

- the simple DO...END sequence – does something just once
- the DO number ... END sequence – does something a fixed number of times
- the DO variable ... END sequence – does something as many times as the number in the variable
- the DO that increments a variable – you can use the variable to access each record in a file or each element in an array
- the DO WHILE – continue doing something as long as a condition is true
- the DO UNTIL – continue doing something until a condition comes true
- the DO FOREVER – continue until you find another way to stop the loop

REXX also has two convenient ways of jumping out of a loop. You don't need to do unstructured things like going to an EXIT or SIGNALling a label.
- -The LEAVE stops the loop in its tracks.
- The ITERATE stops only the current repetition, then goes around one more time.

We'll look at all these variations, one at a time.

Chapter 5: Looping

The simple DO...END sequence.
This isn't really a repetition since it does something just once.
You use it after an IF, an ELSE, or a SELECT's WHEN.
Example:
```
IF A = 1 THEN DO
   SAY "A IS EQUAL TO 1"
   SAY "REALLY EQUAL"
   END
```

The DO number ... END sequence
Example:
```
DO 3
   SAY "CHA"
END
```

The DO variable ... END sequence
Example:
```
TIMES = 4
DO TIMES
   SAY "WOOF"
END
```

Do Practice Problems 23 – 24.

Chapter 5: Looping

The DO that increments a variable
Example:
```
DO INDEX = 1 TO 100
     SAY INDEX
END INDEX
```
This will display the numbers from 1 to 100.
The INDEX on the END instruction is optional, but it is useful when you have nested DO's: it makes REXX check whether the END actually goes with the DO that you think it goes with.

Example, after reading a file with EXECIO (see Chapter 18)
```
DO INDEX = 1 TO RECORD.0
     SAY RECORD.INDEX
END INDEX
```

Example to step through the elements of an array (See Chapter 17 on Compound Variables)
```
DO INDEX = 1 TO 10
   SAY "PLEASE ENTER A NAME"
   PULL ARRAY.INDEX
END INDEX

SAY "THESE ARE THE NAMES YOU ENTERED"

DO INDEX = 1 TO 10
   SAY ARRAY.INDEX
END INDEX
```

This automatically adds 1 to INDEX each time it goes through the loop. You can add a different number: use BY
```
DO INDEX = 1 TO 10 BY 2
   SAY ARRAY.INDEX
END INDEX
```

You can go backwards through the loop by adding a negative number:
```
DO INDEX = 10 TO 1 BY -1
   SAY ARRAY.INDEX
END INDEX
```

Chapter 5: Looping

The DO WHILE
- WHILE continues the loop as long as something is true.
- checks before doing the loop the first time
- may not execute it even once.
- this is like COBOL's PERFORM UNTIL

The generic form of the DO WHILE:
```
DO WHILE something is true
    /* instructions */
END
```

Example:
```
DO WHILE TIME() < "17:01:00"
   SAY "WORK"
END
```

The DO UNTIL
- UNTIL loops up to the moment when something becomes true.
- checks at the END
- doesn't check before the first time.
- will normally do the loop at least once.
- like COBOL's PERFORM UNTIL WITH TEST AFTER

Examples:
```
DO UNTIL TIME() > "17:00:00"
   SAY "WORK"
END

DO UNTIL GUESS = 7
   SAY "WHAT NUMBER AM I THINKING OF (1 - 10)"
   PULL GUESS
END
SAY "THAT'S RIGHT"
```

Chapter 5: Looping

The DO FOREVER
This one is a surprise! I don't know of anything like it in other languages.
It seems odd that a loop would start up without any way to stop! (There are ways to stop it!)

Example that you had better not try:
```
DO FOREVER
      SAY "SEMPER FI"
END
```

Don't let the loop run forever! use one of these four ways to get out of a FOREVER loop:
- **LEAVE** the loop when some condition is true
```
DO FOREVER
      IF TIME() > "17:00:00" THEN LEAVE
END
```

- **SIGNAL** a label when some condition is true (I don't recommend this)
```
DO FOREVER
      IF TIME() > "17:00:00" THEN SIGNAL NEXT
END
NEXT: /* more instructions */
```

- **EXIT** the program when some condition is true
```
DO FOREVER
      IF TIME() > "17:00:00" THEN EXIT
END
```

- Interrupt the program with the PA1 or ATTN key (don't count on it: it doesn't always work under TSO/ISPF).

Chapter 5: Looping

LEAVE
REXX provides a neat, structured way to get out of a loop.
LEAVE gets you out of a repetitive loop. It goes to the END of the loop and then the program keeps going. Your loop is finished.
Example:
```
DO I = 1 TO 10000
   IF I = 200 THEN LEAVE
END I
```

You may specify the variable being incremented on the LEAVE
Example:
```
DO I = 1 TO 10000
   IF I = 200 THEN LEAVE I
END I
```

In a nested loop, LEAVE leaves the loop it's in.
```
DO I = 1 TO 100
    DO J = 1 TO 10
       SAY I J
       IF J = 5 THEN LEAVE   /*finishes J loop */
    END J
END I
```

In a nested loop, you can specify which loop you want to LEAVE.
```
DO I = 1 TO 100
    DO J = 1 TO 10
       SAY I J
       IF J = 5 THEN LEAVE I /*finishes I loop */
    END J
END I
```

Chapter 5: Looping

```
DO I = 1 TO 10

IF I = 1 THEN ITERATE

   SAY I

END I
```

ITERATE: Skipping back to the top of the loop
Few languages provide a convenient means to go back to the beginning of the loop for another go-around. The entire loop is not finished, just this pass through it.

Try this example of skipping "unlucky" 13:
```
DO I = 1 TO 14
    IF I = 13 THEN ITERATE
    SAY "I IS " I
END I
```

You may specify the variable being incremented, on your ITERATE. The I in ITERATE I in this example is not needed.
```
DO I = 1 TO 14
    IF I = 13 THEN ITERATE I
    SAY "I IS " I
END I
```

In a nested loop, you can specify which loop you mean.
```
DO I = 1 TO 30
    DO J = 1 TO 10
       IF J = 5 THEN ITERATE J
       SAY I J
    END J
END I
```

Do Practice Problems 25 – 30.

Chapter 6: SELECT: the CASE Structure

Chapter 6 is about the SELECT verb. SELECT can help you simplify complex conditionals; make your programs easier to understand and more reliable.

Chapter 6 contains:
    Example   60
    Points of syntax   60
    Several instructions: example   61

Chapter 6: SELECT: the CASE Structure

Example

```
SELECT
   WHEN    DATE("B") // 7 = 0      THEN    SAY "MONDAY"
   WHEN    DATE("B") // 7 = 1      THEN    SAY "TUESDAY"
   WHEN    DATE("B") // 7 = 2      THEN    SAY "WEDNESDAY"
   WHEN    DATE("B") // 7 = 3      THEN    SAY "THURSDAY"
   WHEN    DATE("B") // 7 = 4      THEN    SAY "FRIDAY"
   WHEN    DATE("B") // 7 = 5      THEN    SAY "SATURDAY"
   WHEN    DATE("B") // 7 = 6      THEN    SAY "SUNDAY"
 OTHERWISE
     SAY "UNKNOWN DAY"
     SAY "ERROR IN PROGRAM LOGIC"
END  /* goes with SELECT */
/* note DATE("W") also gives you the weekday */
```

SELECT is a good complement to REXX's conditional: **IF**.
While IF can handle only two possibilities: TRUE and FALSE, **SELECT** can handle even more than two.
SELECT is REXX's CASE structure.
Each **WHEN** is tested, one after another. As soon as a **WHEN** is found to be true,
no other **WHEN's** are tested, and control goes after the **END**.

Points of syntax
Note these points of syntax about SELECT:
- `SELECT, WHEN, OTHERWISE, and END`
are separate REXX keywords and must be on separate lines.

- Each **WHEN** introduces a comparison that will be tested.

- You may have as many **WHENs** as you wish.

- Each **WHEN** must have its **THEN**.

- Each **THEN** may have just one instruction, or **DO**...**END** (just like **IF**).

- **OTHERWISE** is required when all the **WHEN's** are false (use it all the time).

- **OTHERWISE** can have more than one instruction, and doesn't require **DO**...**END**!

- The final **END** is required. (It matches the **SELECT**).

Chapter 6: SELECT: the CASE Structure

Several instructions: example

```
DAY = 5  /* or other value*/
SELECT
        WHEN    DAY = 1
        THEN
          DO
            SAY "HAPPY"
            SAY "MONDAY"
          END
        WHEN    DAY = 5
        THEN
          DO
            SAY "TGI"
            SAY "FRIDAY"
          END
        OTHERWISE
          NOP /* no action */
END
```

Putting several instructions after the THEN. If you want to execute more than one instruction after a THEN, bracket them with a DO and an END.

Do Practice Problem 31.

Chapter 7: PARSE

Chapter 7 is about the verb that is the biggest surprise, to those who are new to REXX.
The most powerful and exotic of REXX's verbs is PARSE. It lets you analyze data strings; break them up; search for specific character strings in ways that no other programming language has even thought of. Seeing this verb with all its options at the same time, is confusing. We present the individual features of PARSE here. They are often combined to produce very complex instructions.

Chapter 7 contains:

The basic form of PARSE	64
Origins	65
The Action of PARSE	68
Short forms of PARSE	68
Uses of PARSE: ARG	69
The ARG in a main program	70
The ARG in a user-written function or subroutine	72
Uses of PARSE: PULL	73
Uses of PARSE: EXTERNAL	74
Uses of PARSE: VAR	75
Uses of PARSE: VALUE	76
Uses of PARSE: SOURCE	77
Uses of PARSE: VERSION	79
PARSE Templates: Just Variables	80
PARSE Templates: A Literal	83
PARSE Templates: A Variable in place of a Literal	85
PARSE Templates: Column Delimiting With Numbers	86
Using single numbers	
Using 2 numbers	

Chapter 7: PARSE

The basic form of PARSE is:

```
PARSE [UPPER] origin template
```

The data string is taken from the origin, uppercased if requested, and passed through the template in order to break up the data string into one or more destination variables.

PARSE has no near equivalent in other programming languages. It has some of the features of COBOL UNSTRING but is much more powerful. PARSE breaks up data strings into other, generally shorter, data strings.

The input strings may be delimited by spaces: you are breaking up the strings into several words.

The input strings may be delimited by some character other than spaces, for example, there may be commas or periods where you want to break up the input strings.

The delimiter character may be hard-coded, as in a literal, or it may be in a variable and thus may change from execution to execution.

You may use column positions to delimit data with fixed-length fields. Each field is in a specific column position. You might use this to analyze data fields created by typical business programs.

I will explain PARSE one piece at time on the following pages:
    origins: where the data string being analyzed comes from
    action: what happens during PARSEing
    UPPER: the action of UPPER
    type: each of the 7 types of PARSE
        PARSE: ARG, PULL, EXTERNAL,
        VAR, VALUE, SOURCE, VERSION
    template: what does the template do?
        Various forms of the template: variables, literals, numbers.

Chapter 7: PARSE

Origins

Let's look at the origins of the data strings that PARSE processes.

    ARG – the command line
        ARG refers to the ARGuments or parameters
        on the command line where you execute the REXX program,
        or on the function or subroutine invocation.

        Example of how you execute a program with arguments:
```
==> MYPROG ARG1 ARG2
```

        Example of a PARSE ARG verb in a REXX program:
```
PARSE UPPER ARG VAR1 VAR2
```

    PULL – the terminal and the Internal Data Queue

        – the terminal: you type in data in reply to your program's request.

        – the Internal Data Queue or Stack
            (if you have put anything into it during your program's execution)

        Example of a PARSE PULL verb in a program:
```
Say "Please type in name and phone"
PARSE UPPER PULL NAME PHONE
```
        You then type in your name and phone.

    EXTERNAL – the terminal only

        – the terminal: you type in data in reply to your program's request.

        – this does not look in the Internal Data Queue or Stack
        Example:
```
Say "Please type in name and phone"
PARSE UPPER EXTERNAL NAME PHONE
```
        You then type in your name and phone.

Chapter 7: PARSE

VAR – a variable
    – data is taken from a variable
        PARSE breaks up that variable into several others.

Example of a PARSE VAR verb in a program:
```
VARIABLE = "JOE 4290756"
PARSE UPPER VAR VARIABLE NAME PHONE
```
Note that VARIABLE is the source variable;
NAME and PHONE are the destination variables.

VALUE – a literal or the result of a function

    – data specified in a literal or in a function
        the keyword WITH is required: it shows where the literal ends.

Examples of PARSE VALUE in a program:

```
PARSE UPPER VALUE "JOE 429" WITH NAME PHONE

PARSE UPPER VALUE DATE() WITH DAY MON YEAR
SAY DAY
SAY MON
SAY YEAR
```

SOURCE – internal information from the operating system

Example of a PARSE SOURCE verb in a program:
```
PARSE SOURCE      OP_SYSTEM,
                  HOW_CALLED,
                  EXEC_NAME,
                  DD_NAME,
                  DATASET_NAME AS_CALLED,
                  DEFAULT_ADDRESS,
                  NAME_OF_ADDRESS_SPACE .
Say "op sys  "    OP_SYSTEM
Say "how cal "    HOW_CALLED
Say "exec nam"    EXEC_NAME
Say "dd name "    DD_NAME
Say "dsn as  "    DATASET_NAME AS_CALLED
Say "def adr "    DEFAULT_ADDRESS
Say "addrspc "    NAME_OF_ADDRESS_SPACE
```

Chapter 7: PARSE

VERSION – the version/release of REXX

Example of a PARSE VERSION verb in a program:
```
PARSE VERSION LANGUAGE LEVEL DATE
Say Language
Say Level
Say Date
```
This might produce the result:
```
REXX370
3.48
01 May 1992
```

Chapter 7: PARSE

The Action of PARSE

What happens during PARSEing. Data strings are read from the origin (see above for origins). Data is passed through the template (explained below) and is assigned to the destination variable(s) according to the rules used in the template.
All of the destination variables are affected in some way – even if it means that they are assigned only the null string (zero characters).

The origin variable(s) are not changed unless one of them also appears among the destination variables.

Short forms of PARSE
PARSE is a REXX keyword, or verb. In its full form, the word PARSE is always used. Sometimes, however it may be left out for convenience:

Full form of PARSE.	Shortened form
`PARSE UPPER ARG variable...`	`ARG variable...`
`PARSE UPPER PULL variable...`	`PULL variable..`
`PARSE UPPER VAR VAR1 VAR1`	`UPPER VAR1`

The option keyword UPPER will convert to upper case. If you omit UPPER, the data is not converted to upper case. Be aware of this in comparisons. If the data is mixed case, your comparison literals must be mixed case as well.
However, the short forms ARG and PULL convert to upper case.

Example:
```
Say "Please type in your name"
PARSE PULL NAME /* person types in Ellen */
If Name = "ELLEN" then say "Hello"
/* will not find Ellen, but will find ELLEN*/
```

Chapter 7: PARSE

Uses of PARSE: ARG

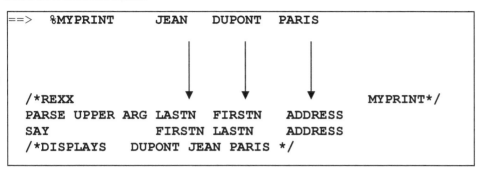

```
==>   %MYPRINT     JEAN    DUPONT   PARIS


/*REXX                                        MYPRINT*/
PARSE UPPER ARG LASTN   FIRSTN   ADDRESS
SAY             FIRSTN  LASTN    ADDRESS
/*DISPLAYS   DUPONT JEAN PARIS */
```

PARSE UPPER ARG receives information from the command line. The symbol ==> shows what was keyed in at the terminal.

ARG or PARSE [UPPER] ARG is used to receive information typed in at the command line when the program is executed. In the example above, MYPRINT is the name of the program; JEAN   DUPONT   PARIS is the data typed in after the program name. That data is placed into the variables on the PARSE UPPER ARG statement in the program.

The **ARG** or **PARSE [UPPER] ARG** statement may appear in a main program or in a subroutine or in a function. The above example illustrates a main program. There is one difference in the way they are used in those two places: whether you use commas or not. More about that on the following pages.

Chapter 7: PARSE

The ARG in a main program, (not a subroutine/function).
A main program is one that is executed from one of the following:

- Native or Line Mode TSO. (no commas between arguments)
    Ex: `PROGNAME or %PROGNAME arg1 arg2`

- option 6 of ISPF (no commas between arguments)
    Ex: `PROGNAME or %PROGNAME arg1 arg2`

- the command line within ISPF (no commas between arguments)
    Ex: `TSO PROGNAME or TSO %PROGNAME arg1 arg2`

- the command line within the ISPF Editor (no commas)
    Ex: `TSO PROGNAME or TSO %PROGNAME arg1 arg2`

- from an ISPF panel's internal coding
    (beyond the scope of this book)

- from within another REXX program (no commas between arguments)
    executed like this:
    `"PROGNAME" arg1 arg2 "`
    or
    `"%PROGNAME" arg1 arg2 "`
    or
    `"EXEC pds-name(membername) " 'arg1 arg2 ' EXEC"`

- from within a TSO CLIST (no commas between arguments)
    executed like this:
    `PROGNAME arg1 arg2`
    or
    `%PROGNAME arg1 arg2`
    or
    `EXEC pds-name(membername) 'arg1 arg2 ' EXEC`

> ARG does not work with Editor macros.

Chapter 7: PARSE

The ARG in a main program, continued
In all these cases just shown just above, your ARG or PARSE ARG may not separate the variables with commas. Separate them with spaces.

How you actually execute the main program using the ARG values
In each case just shown above, you may place the values (arguments) for your ARG variables right after the command that executes the program, on the same line (known generally as the command line).
Do not separate the values with commas. Commas do not have any special meaning on the command line.
Separate the parameters with spaces.

These examples show what is typed *on the command line*, not what *is in the program*.

```
TSO PROGNAME arg1 arg2
TSO %PROGNAME arg1 arg2
"PROGNAME" arg1 arg2
"%PROGNAME" arg1 arg2
"EXEC 'pds-name(membername)' 'arg1 arg2' EXEC"
```

ARG is generally placed first in a program, right after the initial comment.
It doesn't have to be first.
It may be anywhere in the program.
You may have more than one **ARG** statement – each one will read the same data.
There are no commas between the variables in an **ARG** statement in a main program.

Chapter 7: PARSE

The ARG in a user-written function or subroutine.

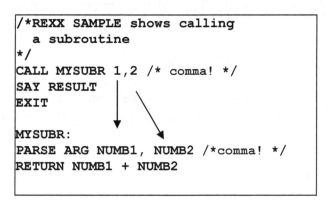

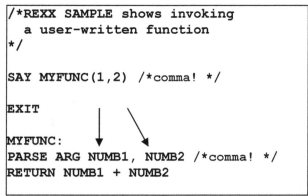

This works like the **PARSE ARG** in a main program shown a few pages back except for the commas. The commas work here when used between variables. In fact, I strongly advise you to use commas here because the IBM built-in functions all use commas.
This will give you more consistency in your programs.

The above two examples show a user-written function and a user-written subroutine that are internal to the program that calls them. Chapter 14 will show you how to write those internal functions/subroutines while Chapter 15 will show you how to write internal subroutines.

Commas may be used the same way in internal functions/subroutines as well as external functions/subroutines.

Chapter 7: PARSE

Uses of PARSE: PULL

```
SAY "PLEASE ENTER YOUR NAME"
PARSE PULL NAME
SAY "THANK YOU, "   NAME
SAY " FOR ENTERING YOUR NAME "
```

The **PARSE PULL** (or PULL) takes its input data from one or both of the following: the Internal Data Queue (the Stack) or the keyboard.

If there is nothing in the Internal Data Queue the keyboard and terminal will unlock and wait for you to type in something.

PARSE PULL is the normal way to do terminal dialogue (if there is nothing in the Internal Data Queue). Just be sure to do a SAY first, to tell the user what to type in!
```
    SAY "PLEASE ENTER YOUR NAME"
    PARSE PULL NAME
    SAY "THANK YOU, "   NAME
    SAY " FOR ENTERING YOUR NAME "
```

Try this example on your system. It puts something into the Internal Data Queue, so the **PARSE PULL** will take its input from there, not from the keyboard.
```
    Push "Clarabelle" /*put word in the Data Queue*/
    SAY "PLEASE ENTER YOUR NAME"
    PARSE PULL NAME
    SAY "THANK YOU, "   NAME
    SAY " FOR ENTERING YOUR NAME "
```

PARSE PULL will not convert to upper case
PARSE UPPER PULL will convert to upper case
PULL will convert to upper case.

Do Practice Problem 32.

Chapter 7: PARSE

Uses of PARSE: EXTERNAL

```
Push "Clarabelle"  /*put something
into the data queue*/

SAY "PLEASE ENTER YOUR NAME"
PARSE EXTERNAL NAME
SAY "THANK YOU, "   NAME
SAY " FOR ENTERING YOUR NAME"
```

PARSE EXTERNAL takes from terminal but not from the Internal Data Queue.
If there is already something in the Internal Data Queue, you may avoid disturbing it by using **PARSE EXTERNAL**.
This may come in handy if you are putting lines of data into the Internal Data Queue for later use in a file writing statement, and need to ask the user for something.
You may totally bypass everything that is in the Internal Data Queue by using **PARSE EXTERNAL**.

The above example contains a surprise! The word Clarabelle is still in the Internal Data Queue when the program ends.
The system treats this as if you had actually typed in Clarabelle: it is treated as a command that you had typed in!
Luckily Clarabelle is not a real command and will cause an error message, with no harm done.
However, if you had put a real system command into the Internal Data Queue it would have been executed!
More about all this in Chapter 16 on the Internal Data Queue.

PARSE EXTERNAL will not convert to upper case
PARSE UPPER EXTERNAL will convert to upper case.

Chapter 7: PARSE

Uses of PARSE: VAR

```
NAME = "CAL A. MAZOO"
  PARSE VAR NAME    FIRST MIDDLE LAST
  SAY "YOUR MIDDLE INITIAL IS " MIDDLE
```

PARSE VAR splits the contents of a variable into one or more other variables. What is strange about the syntax of this PARSE is that the variable that is being **PARSEd** comes right after the word **VAR** and before the target variables.

The syntax of this **PARSE** does not make it clear that the data in **NAME** is broken up and placed in the variables **FIRST, MIDDLE** and **LAST**.
```
  NAME = "CAL A. MAZOO"
  PARSE VAR NAME    FIRST MIDDLE LAST
  SAY "YOUR MIDDLE INITIAL IS " MIDDLE
```

You may make the syntax a little clearer by putting the source variable and the target variables on separate lines, using a comma to show continuation.
```
  NAME = "CAL A. MAZOO"
  PARSE VAR NAME,
        FIRST MIDDLE LAST
  SAY "YOUR MIDDLE INITIAL IS " MIDDLE
```

PARSE VAR can be really useful in reading files. After reading a record the contents of the record are in a variable, **RECORD.1** in the example. The record is broken up into 4 separate words.
```
     /* after reading, RECORD.1 contains a record*/
     PARSE VAR RECORD.1 NAME ADDRESS PHONE E_MAIL
```

PARSE VAR will not convert to upper case
PARSE UPPER VAR will convert to upper case.

Chapter 7: PARSE

Uses of PARSE: VALUE

PARSE VALUE is used when there is data in a literal string or is the result of a function and you want to break it up into variables.

The usefulness of breaking up a literal string stretches the imagination. You will more than likely use this to break up the result of a function, whether built-in or user-written.

The keyword **WITH** is required. Otherwise REXX couldn't tell where the target variables begin.

```
PARSE VALUE "THIS IS A SAMPLE" WITH A B C D
Say A
Say B
Say C
Say D
PARSE VALUE DATE() WITH DAY MONTH YEAR
Say day
Say month
Say year
```

You may make the syntax a little clearer by putting the instruction and the target variables on separate lines, using a comma to show continuation.

```
PARSE VALUE "THIS IS A SAMPLE",
     WITH A B C D
Say A
Say B
Say C
Say D
```

PARSE VALUE will not convert to upper case
PARSE UPPER VALUE will convert to upper case.

Chapter 7: PARSE

Uses of PARSE: SOURCE

Your program may execute in different environments. It may work in some environments and not work in others or may work differently. In each case you will want to know what environment you are running in.
PARSE SOURCE tells you how the program was executed and environmental information.
The example refers to REXX under TSO.

```
        PARSE SOURCE        OP_SYSTEM,
                            HOW_CALLED,
                            EXEC_NAME,
                            DD_NAME,
                            DATASET_NAME AS_CALLED,
                            DEFAULT_ADDRESS,
                            NAME_OF_ADDRESS_SPACE .
        Say "op sys  "      OP_SYSTEM
        Say "how cal "      HOW_CALLED
        Say "exec nam"      EXEC_NAME
        Say "dd name "      DD_NAME
        Say "dsn as  "      DATASET_NAME AS_CALLED
        Say "def adr "      DEFAULT_ADDRESS
        Say "addrspc "      NAME_OF_ADDRESS_SPACE
```

Chapter 7: PARSE

Here's what the variables mean, under TSO:

OP_SYSTEM	`TSO (the literal TSO)`

HOW_CALLED	`COMMAND, SUBROUTINE (CALL),`
	`or FUNCTION`
	`(invoked like this: Funname().`

EXEC_NAME	`Member name of the Exec.`

DD_NAME	`SYSEXEC or SYSPROC.`
	`when called implicitly`
	`(by member name).`
	`unpredictable DDNAME`
	`when called explicitly (EXEC…).`

DATASET_NAME	`Name of PDS the program`
	`was in.`
	`when called explicitly.`
	`? when called implicitly.`

AS_CALLED	`normally a ?`
DEFAULT_ADDRESS	`the initial address` `environment TSO`
NAME_OF_ADDRESS_SPACE	`TSO, MVS, or ISPF.`
.	`period in the last position` `is a dummy variable`

The variable OP_SYSTEM will return different things under different operating systems: 'TSO' on TSO; OS/2 on OS/2; CMS on CMS.

Chapter 7: PARSE

Uses of PARSE: VERSION

`PARSE VERSION` will tell you the version of REXX you are using.
This may be of value if you are using features that work only in certain versions of REXX.

```
PARSE VERSION LANGUAGE LEVEL DAY MONTH YEAR
SAY "MY LEVEL OF REXX IS " LEVEL
SAY "CREATED " DAY MONTH YEAR
```

Might produce the following results on TSO:

```
LANGUAGE IS REXX370
MY LEVEL OF REXX IS  3.48
CREATED   01 May 1992
```

Chapter 7: PARSE

PARSE Templates: Just Variables: Same number of words as variables

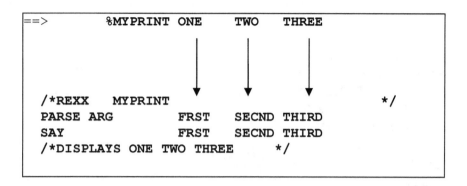

Same number of words as variables.
The template in **PARSE** is what controls the splitting up of data. We'll look at the simplest template first: the one that contains just variables.
Please note that it doesn't matter what the origin of the data was (see the preceding pages for the origins). The data is split according to the rules of the template regardless of the origin of the data. So **PARSE ARG** and **PARSE PULL** and the others all split data up by the rules of the template.

When the template consists of just variables the main rule is simple: Data is broken up by words. When there are three words in the input and three variables in the **PARSE** each word goes into one variable. This is very simple and neat.

It's not always that simple and neat, however: there can be:
- the same number of words in the input data as there are variables in the **PARSE** (see the example at the top of this page)
- more words than variables (see below)
- more variables than words (see below).

Chapter 7: PARSE

PARSE Templates: Just Variables: More words than variables

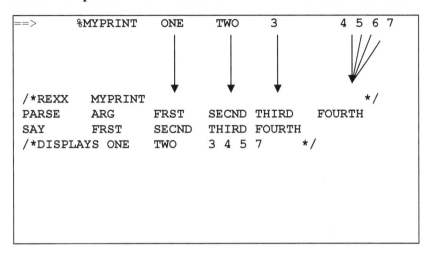

More words than variables.
When the input data contains more words than there are variables to hold them, the extra words go into the last variable.
In the above example 4, 5, 6 and 7 go into the variable "FOURTH".
Nothing is lost with REXX!
This also means: if you just have only one variable all the words go into that variable.

Dropping extra words.
If you don't want those extra words in your input data you can drop them. Just use a period instead of a variable. It acts like a dummy variable: data goes in but it never comes out, just like a black hole absorbs light.

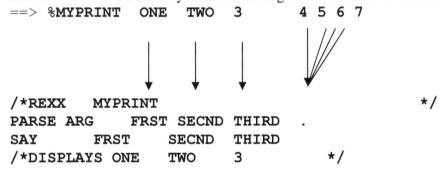

The period may be used to just drop a word: This will drop the second word:
`PARSE ARG FRST . THIRD`

Chapter 7: PARSE

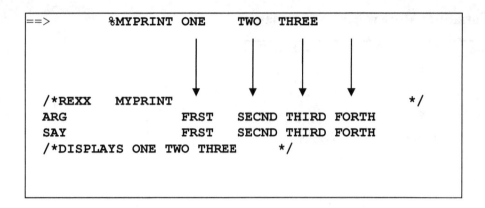

More variables than words.
When you don't have enough words in the input for all the variables, the extra variables are made null.
All target variables in the parse template are changed in some way.
FORTH, in the above example, is made null (zero characters.)

Chapter 7: PARSE

PARSE Templates: A Literal

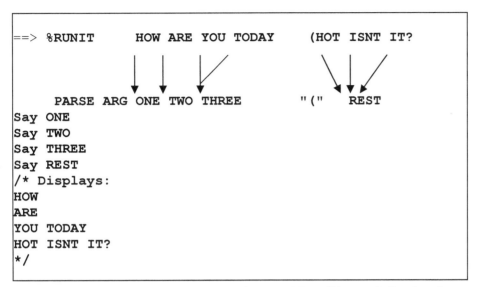

If you use a literal string in a PARSE template REXX will search for the character string in the input data. "(" is the literal string in the above example.

Found
Here is what happens if REXX finds the character string.
It splits the input data into two distinct parts: the part before the found character string and the part after the character string.
It then performs, in effect two different PARSEs.
- First on the left, totally ignoring the string on the right. The rules of a simple PARSE are followed for the input data on the left.
- Then on the right, totally ignoring the string on the left. The rules of a simple PARSE are followed for the input data on the right.

The literal character string is not placed in the target variables.

Not found
If the literal character string is not found in the input data, REXX acts as if the literal string were found in the last character position of the input data: I.E. at the extreme right.
It then performs, in effect two different PARSEs.
- It PARSEs the input data into the target variables at the left of the literal string.
- It sets the target variables at the right of the literal string to null.

Chapter 7: PARSE

```
/* REXX sample breaks up name into levels of
qualification*/

DSN = "TRAIN01.ABC.COBOL(PROG1)"

PARSE VAR DSN LIBRARY "(" MEMBER ")"

PARSE VAR LIBRARY QUAL1 "." QUAL2 "." QUAL3 "." QUAL4

SAY "THE LIBRARY NAME WAS " LIBRARY
SAY "THE MEMBER NAME WAS  " MEMBER
SAY "QUALIFIER 1 " QUAL1 /* TRAIN01 */
SAY "QUALIFIER 2 " QUAL2 /* ABC     */
SAY "QUALIFIER 3 " QUAL3 /* COBOL   */
SAY "QUALIFIER 4 " QUAL4 /*         */
```

Breaking up a dataset name (TSO only)

The example above shows something useful that you can do on TSO. The example applies only on TSO because of the structure of the dataset name. However, the principle can be applied to any type of data string on any system.

The period in the quotes makes **PARSE** break up the dataset name, dividing it at each period. The example shows 3 periods, so it can handle only four levels of qualification.

The parentheses in the example above make **PARSE** separate the member name from the full dataset name. If there is no member name and no parenthesis, the variable **MEMBER** will be null.

Chapter 7: PARSE

PARSE Templates: A Variable in place of a Literal

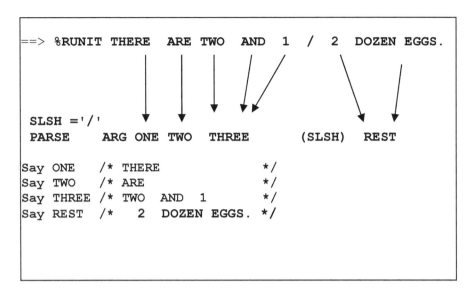

The previous page showed the use of a literal in a PARSE template. There are times when a literal isn't what you need: you need to change the character string in the literal. Using a variable instead of a literal allows you to do this. The only restriction is that *this variable must be in parentheses*, to distinguish it from the target variables.

The following example shows how you might pick up the first character in a data string and use that character as a delimiter later on in the same instruction.

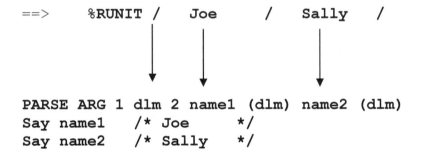

```
PARSE ARG 1 dlm 2 name1 (dlm) name2 (dlm)
Say name1    /* Joe    */
Say name2    /* Sally  */
```

Chapter 7: PARSE

PARSE Templates: Column Delimiting With Numbers

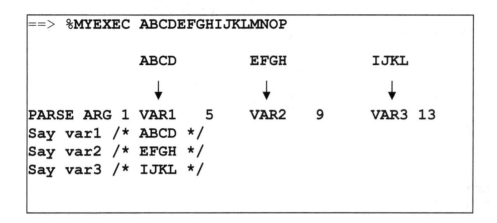

If you know the exact column position at which you want to break up the input string, you can specify the column numbers (but read on... there's a little trick).

You can use single numbers, as in the example above. You can also use 2 numbers as shown on the next page.

Using single numbers
When you use numbers, spaces between words do not mean anything. You are no longer breaking up by words; you are breaking apart at specific column positions.
The trick is this. The number at the left of a variable is the starting position of the variable's data. So VAR1 has a 1 at its left. This means that VAR1's data starts at column position 1. VAR2 starts at column 5. VAR3 starts at column 9.

So where does VAR1's data end? At column 4. Not 5. 5 is where VAR2 starts!

VAR1 gets columns 1 through 4
VAR2 gets columns 5 through 8
VAR3 gets columns 9 through 12

The rule (the trick) can be expressed this way: Look at a variable
- the number on the left is the start column
- the number on the right, minus 1, is the end column.

Chapter 7: PARSE

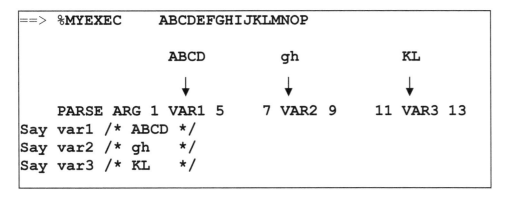

Using 2 numbers
If you use two numbers in your template you can skip columns in the input data and you can put the same columns into two different target variables.

Good news! The rule for this is the same as for single numbers (previous page).
The rule (the trick) can be expressed this way: Look at a variable
- the number on the left is the start column
- the number on the right, minus 1, is the end column.

Columns are skipped in the above example,
VAR1 gets columns 1 through 4
VAR2 gets columns 7 through 8
VAR3 gets columns 11 through 12

The same data is put into two variables VAR1 and VAR3. The following example puts columns 1 through 2 into VAR1 and VAR3.

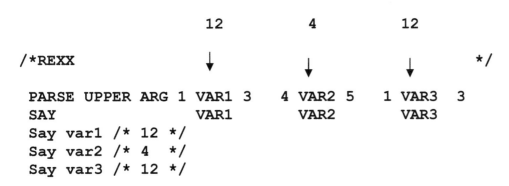

Do Practice Problems 33 – 41.

Chapter 8: Debugging

Chapter 8 is about watching your program run, seeing just where the flow of execution goes, and examining the variables as they change.
REXX lets you display anything and everything as your program runs.
You can interact with your program as it runs with Interactive Debugging. Watch your program run!

Chapter 8 contains:
    Interactive Debug   90
        What you can do during Interactive Debug   90
        Turning on Interactive Debug   91
        Codes displayed during Interactive Debug   92
    Tracing: the Smaller Guns   93
    Combinations of the TRACE verb   94

Chapter 8: Debugging

Interactive Debug

> **What you can do during interactive debug**
>
> Execute the next instruction by pressing ENTER.
> Reexecute the last instruction that executed by typing "=".
> Display and change variables.
> Issue commands to TSO
> End the program by typing **EXIT**.
> Display a line of your program with the SOURCELINE
>   function: `SAY SOURCELINE(line number)`
> Display the source program (typed all on one line).
>   `DO I = 1 TO 9999;SAY SOURCELINE(I);END`
> Change 9999 to the last line number that you want displayed.

REXX has a truly useful debugging capability. Interactive Debugging is the most powerful. Less powerful forms of debugging and tracing will be shown on the following pages.

When you are in Interactive Debug, you are talking directly to the REXX interpreter: everything you type in is processed as if it were a line in your program.
REXX interprets it and executes it immediately. Anything you can do in your program you can do in Interactive Debug.

You can set variables, display them, try out a REXX instruction to see what it does.
The only thing you can't do is change your source program.

It does produce a lot of output which takes a bit of getting used to. You will probably turn on Interactive Debug only in the parts of your program that need it.

Chapter 8: Debugging

> **Turning on Interactive Debug**
>
> in the program
>   TRACE ?R   (most common)
>   TRACE ?I   (the full monty)
>
> before executing your program (on TSO)
>   EXECUTIL TS
>
> during execution
>   press PA1/ATTN,
>   then type TS (Trace Start)

You can turn on Interactive Debug any of the ways shown above. The most common way is by putting **TRACE ?R** in your program at the spot where you want to turn on Interactive Debug.

Using **EXECUTIL TS** is less common. You would type it on the command line before executing your program (prefixed by 'TSO' if on an ISPF panel).

If you realize you need the big gun of Interactive Debug after you start your program, you can turn on Interactive Debug while your program is running: press PA1 or ATTN (actual key name depends on terminal emulator). Then type **TS** to start trace. (If you type **HI** for Halt Interpretation you will cancel the program and go to any **HALT** trap you may have set up). See Chapter 9.

Chapter 8: Debugging

Codes displayed during Interactive Debug
REXX displays these codes during Interactive Debug. They tell you just what the display means.

```
*-* Original program line.

+++ Trace message.

>>> Result of an expression.  During TRACE R.

>.> Value assigned to a placeholder (period)
    during Parsing.

>C> The resolved name of a compound variable.

>F> Result of a function call.

>L> A literal.

>O> Result of an operation on two terms.

>P> Result of a prefix operation.

>V> Contents of a variable.
```

Chapter 8: Debugging

Tracing: the Smaller Guns

Combinations of the TRACE verb
You may not need Interactive Debug. You may find that one of the following will give you what you want. This list shows all practical combinations.

```
TRACE    !             Nothing traced,
                       Don't execute TSO commands

TRACE    O (Off)       Nothing traced

TRACE    N (Normal)    TSO cmds that fail/error out
                       (The default)
                       REXX verbs that fail

TRACE    F (Failure)   TSO commands that don't exist,
                       or abend.

TRACE    E (Error)     TSO commands that don't work

TRACE    !C            Trace TSO commands,
                       But don't execute them

TRACE    C (Commands)  TSO commands

TRACE    L (Labels)    Labels only

TRACE    A (All)       Labels
                       Commands
                       REXX verbs
```

More on the next page...

Chapter 8: Debugging

Combinations of the TRACE verb, continued

```
TRACE !R (Results)   Labels
                     Commands
                     REXX verbs
                     Any time a variable changes
                     Don't execute TSO commands


TRACE  R (Results)   Labels
                     Commands
                     REXX verbs
                     any time a variable changes


TRACE ?R (Results)   Labels
                     Commands
                     REXX verbs
                     Any time a variable changes
                     With Interactive Debug


TRACE  I (Intermed)  Labels
                     Commands
                     REXX verbs
                     Any time a variable changes
                     Intermediate results
                     Example: C = (4*3) + 2


TRACE !I (Intermed)  Labels
                     Commands
                     REXX verbs
                     Any time a variable changes
                     Intermediate results
                     Example: C = (4*3) + 2
                     Don't execute TSO commands


TRACE ?I (Intermed)  Labels
                     Commands
                     REXX verbs
                     Any time a variable changes
                     Intermediate results
                     Example: C = (4*3) + 2
                     With Interactive Debug
```

Chapter 9: Trapping Unexpected Conditions

Chapter 9 is about what you can do when something unexpected happens.
I judge a program by what it does when something goes wrong. If it truly messes up, it is not a very smart program. Exception traps allow you to regain control in your program when something happens...

Chapter 9 contains:

Situations you might want to trap	96
Trapping Unexpected Conditions: General	97
The trap that terminates	97
The trap that continues	97
Changing the name of the trap	98
Trapping Unexpected Conditions: Syntax	99
Trapping Unexpected Conditions: Error	100
Trapping Unexpected Conditions: Failure	102
Trapping Unexpected Conditions: Novalue	103
Trapping Unexpected Conditions: Halt	104
Trapping Unexpected Conditions: Contents of the Trap	105

Chapter 9: Trapping Unexpected Conditions

Situations you might want to trap	
SYNTAX:	REXX syntax errors recommend you not trap
ERROR:	TSO/ISPF commands that don't work properly. (RC > 0)
FAILURE:	commands that don't exist, or that abend. (RC < 0, or abend code) recommend you omit; ERROR will then include this one
NOVALUE:	using uninitialized variables. recommend you not trap
HALT:	the user pressing the PA1 or ATTN keys. you may want to trap in order to do cleanup

Programs don't always do what you want them to. The user doesn't always type in reasonable input. The situation in the operating system may not be what you expect: files may be missing; you may not get the syntax of TSO commands correct.

You may put exception traps in your program to intercept unusual conditions and take appropriate action.

If you set up an exception trap you can regain control of your program when a situation arises. The next page shows a generic form of the trap.

Chapter 9: Trapping Unexpected Conditions

Trapping Unexpected Conditions: General

```
         The Trap that Terminates

SIGNAL ON condition

/* other instructions */

EXIT

condition:
/* handle condition */
/* other instructions */

EXIT
```

```
         The Trap that Continues

CALL    ON condition

/* other instructions */

EXIT

condition:
/* handle condition */
/* other instructions */

RETURN
```

There are two kinds of trap:
    The trap that terminates
    The trap that continues

The trap that terminates is activated by **SIGNAL** in the main part of the program.
The actual trap is located physically at the end of the program, after an **EXIT**.
The trap must end with an **EXIT**.
SIGNAL is a **GO TO**: you can't come back in **REXX**!

The trap that continues is activated by **CALL** in the main part of the program.
The actual trap is located physically at the end of the program, after an **EXIT**.
The trap must end with an **RETURN**. **CALL** implies that you are coming back.

Chapter 9: Trapping Unexpected Conditions

Changing the name of the trap. The trap normally has the same name as the exception that it traps, so an error trap is named **ERROR:** with a colon, as in all REXX labels. You can use a different name if you wish. Just use the **NAME** keyword on the **SIGNAL** or **CALL** followed by the desired name, as in the following two examples:

```
SIGNAL   ON exception   NAME routine_name
/* other instructions */

EXIT

routine_name:
/* handle exception */
/* other instructions */

EXIT
```


```
CALL   ON exception   NAME routine_name
/* other instructions */

EXIT

routine_name:
/* handle exception */
/* other instructions */
```

RETURN

Chapter 9: Trapping Unexpected Conditions

Trapping Unexpected Conditions: Syntax

```
                        A Syntax Trap
/* REXX Syntax*/
SIGNAL ON SYNTAX

   SAY "A" - "B"
   EXIT

   SYNTAX:
   SAY "SYNTAX ERROR"
   SAY "ERROR ON LINE " SIGL
   SAY "LINE WITH ERROR IS "          SOURCELINE(SIGL)
   SAY "ERROR MESSAGE FROM REXX IS " ERRORTEXT(RC)
   EXIT
```

Specific examples of the trap: THE SYNTAX TRAP

What triggers the **SYNTAX** trap?
    a REXX syntax error
    CALLing a bogus function or subroutine
    Examples:
```
        Say "A" - "B"
        X = (Cur - Prev / Prev
        Call Notthere
```

What happens if you don't use a **SYNTAX** trap?
    REXX displays an error message and the line of code that caused the problem,
    then it cancels the program.

What can you do with a **SYNTAX** trap?
    you can display only what you want to, hiding REXX messages if you wish,
    but you still have to terminate the program.

You should terminate the program after a syntax error, so use **SIGNAL**,
not **CALL**, and end with an **EXIT**.
SIGNAL OFF SYNTAX turns off the trap.

Chapter 9: Trapping Unexpected Conditions

Trapping Unexpected Conditions: Error

```
                        An ERROR Trap
/* REXX Errortr*/
SIGNAL ON ERROR      /* this trap terminates*/
"LISTALC JUNK"       /* TSO command set up wrong*/


EXIT

ERROR:
SAY "COMMAND FAILED"
SAY "ERROR ON LINE " SIGL
SAY "LINE CONTAINING ERROR IS "    SOURCELINE(SIGL)
SAY "THE PROBLEM IS IN:"           CONDITION("D")
SAY RC " WAS RETURN CODE FROM TSO COMMAND"
EXIT
```

Specific examples of the trap: THE ERROR TRAP

What triggers the **ERROR** trap?
    a known TSO or ISPF command works wrong
    a TSO or ISPF command gives a non-zero return code
    Examples:
        `"LISTALC JUNK"`
        `"DELETE NONE.SUCH"`

What happens if you don't use an **ERROR** trap?
REXX pays no attention to the situation. Program continues undaunted, merrily giving non-zero `RC's`.
later TSO/ISPF commands may fail as well

What can you do with an **ERROR** trap?
    you can terminate the program
    you can correct the situation and continue with the program
        use `CALL + RETURN` instead of `SIGNAL + EXIT`
    you can display warning messages

If you have no **FAILURE** trap but you have an **ERROR** trap, **ERROR** takes the place of **FAILURE**.
`SIGNAL OFF ERROR` turns off the trap.

Chapter 9: Trapping Unexpected Conditions

Trapping Unexpected Conditions: Error

The ERROR trap that continues.

The example shown on the previous page shows an **ERROR** trap that terminates. Sometimes you will want to continue with your program after an **ERROR** exception.

Use a trap with **CALL**.

Example:
```
/* Rexx Errortr*/
CALL    ON ERROR
"LISTALC JUNK"
/* Program flow continues here */

EXIT

ERROR:
SAY "COMMAND FAILED"
SAY "ERROR ON LINE " SIGL
SAY "LINE CONTAINING ERROR IS "    SOURCELINE(SIGL)
SAY "THE PROBLEM IS IN:"           CONDITION("D")
SAY RC " WAS RETURN CODE FROM TSO COMMAND"
RETURN
```

Chapter 9: Trapping Unexpected Conditions

Trapping Unexpected Conditions: Failure

```
/* Rexx Fail*/
SIGNAL ON FAILURE
   "THIS IS NOT A TSO CMD"
   "LISTDOG"
   "CALL 'BADLUCK.LIB(BOOM)'"  /* abends */

   EXIT

   FAILURE:   SAY "COMMAND FAILED "
   SAY "ERROR ON LINE " SIGL
   SAY "LINE CONTAINING ERROR IS "    SOURCELINE(SIGL)
   SAY "THE PROBLEM IS IN:"           CONDITION("D")
   SAY RC " WAS RETURN CODE FROM TSO COMMAND"
   SAY D2X(ABS(RC)) "IS SYSTEM ABEND CODE"
   EXIT
```

Specific examples of the trap: THE FAILURE TRAP

What triggers the **FAILURE** trap?
    a unknown TSO or ISPF command
    a TSO or ISPF command or program which abends
    Examples:
        `"THIS IS NOT A TSO CMD"`
        `"LISTDOG"`
        `"CALL 'BADLUCK.LIB(BOOM)'"`

> CALL in quotes is the TSO command that executes a compiled program

What happens if you don't use a **FAILURE** trap or an **ERROR** trap?
REXX pays no attention to the situation. Program continues undaunted...
later TSO/ISPF commands may fail as well

What can you do with a **FAILURE** trap?
    you can terminate the program
    you can correct the situation and continue with the program
        use **CALL + RETURN** instead of **SIGNAL + EXIT**
    you can display warning messages.

If you have no **FAILURE** trap but you have an **ERROR** trap, **ERROR** takes the place of **FAILURE**.
SIGNAL OFF FAILURE turns off the trap.

Chapter 9: Trapping Unexpected Conditions

Trapping Unexpected Conditions: Novalue

```
SIGNAL ON NOVALUE
   SAY HELLO

   EXIT

   NOVALUE:
   SAY "PLEASE DEFINE YOUR VARIABLES"
   SAY "ERROR ON LINE " SIGL
   SAY "LINE CONTAINING ERROR IS "    SOURCELINE(SIGL)
   SAY "THE PROBLEM IS IN:"           CONDITION("D")
   EXIT
```

Specific examples of the trap: THE NOVALUE TRAP

What triggers the **NOVALUE** trap?
      using a variable that was not initialized
      Example:
          SAY HELLO

What happens if you don't use a **NOVALUE**?
Nothing serious.
The variable is taken as a literal containing its name, but uppercased

What can you do with a **NOVALUE** trap?
      you can terminate the program
      you can display a message saying that you shouldn't do that.

You can terminate the program or continue if you wish.

SIGNAL OFF NOVALUE turns off the trap.

Chapter 9: Trapping Unexpected Conditions

Trapping Unexpected Conditions: Halt

```
SIGNAL ON HALT
/* Intervening instructions */
   EXIT

   HALT:
   SAY "DON'T INTERRUPT"
   SAY "PROGRAM WAS ON LINE " SIGL
   SAY "LINE CONTENTS "    SOURCELINE(SIGL)
   EXIT
```

What triggers the **HALT** trap?
    pressing PA1 or ATTN while the program is running
    then typing **HI** (Halt Interpretation)
    (Find out what Windows keys these are mapped to on your computer)

What happens if you don't use a **HALT** trap?
A PA1 or ATTN will (sometimes) terminate your program
Note that on TSO the results are unpredictable.

What can you do with a **HALT** trap?
    you can terminate the program
    you can clean up and terminate the program
    you can continue with the program
        use **CALL + RETURN** instead of **SIGNAL + EXIT**
    you can display a message.
    It's not a good idea to prevent the user from canceling the program.

Warning: TSO does not always handle interrupts properly. Expect the worst.

SIGNAL OFF HALT turns off the trap.

Chapter 9: Trapping Unexpected Conditions

Trapping Unexpected Conditions: Contents of the Trap

```
                    What you can put in the trap.
label:
 SAY "ERROR ON LINE " SIGL
 SAY "LINE CONTAINING ERROR IS "   SOURCELINE(SIGL)
 SAY "THE PROBLEM IS IN:"          CONDITION("D")
 SAY "ERROR MESSAGE FROM REXX IS " ERRORTEXT(RC)
 SAY RC " WAS RETURN CODE FROM TSO COMMAND"
 /* next is for FAILURE trap only: */
 SAY D2X(ABS(RC)) "IS SYSTEM ABEND CODE"
 EXIT
```

You can use any of the following in your exception trap:

- any REXX instruction/TSO command

- SIGL: line number that sent control to the trap

- The function SOURCELINE(SIGL):
-       shows the actual program statement

- The function ERRORTEXT(RC): is the REXX error message

- The function CONDITION("D") shows the string in error

- RC contains the return code from TSO commands

- in a Failure trap the function D2X(ABS(RC)) shows the system abend code.

Do Practice Problem 42.

Chapter 10: SIGNAL: the Extinct "GO TO"

Chapter 10 is about a REXX verb that can be misused. I suggest you use it only to exit the program after a fatal error.

After working on ancient, rusty, leaky, unreliable old programs that used GO TO everywhere they could, I came to appreciate structured programming.

REXX reluctantly allows you to GO somewhere. You have to pay a penalty: you can't come back.

Chapter 10 contains:
    Signal: go there (but don't come back)   108

Chapter 10: SIGNAL: the Extinct "GO TO"

Signal: go there (but don't come back)

```
SIGNAL THE_END
/* code */


THE_END:
/* code */

EXIT
```

The "GO TO" is hidden in REXX's SIGNAL instruction. The author of REXX and I are both proponents of structured programming. We don't like "GO TO's". But we use them when we need a quick way to bail out of our program without any formality.

SIGNAL label sends you somewhere else in your program. But if you want a program that is readable and easy on the brain matter, you'll use very few SIGNALs!

Signal is not the best way to build your program's logic. If you use SIGNAL to go somewhere inside of, or to leave a logic construct (IF, DO, etc) SIGNAL kills the logic construct and your program won't work right.

Chapter 10: SIGNAL: the Extinct "GO TO"

If you try the following example you'll see how **SIGNAL** kills the **DO** loop. The **DO** loop stops working!

```
/* REXX shows how a SIGNAL destroys
    a loop control structure         */
 Say "BEGIN"
 Do I = 1 TO 5
   Say I
   If I = 2 then SIGNAL NEXT
   Say "A"
   NEXT:
   Say "B"
 End
 Say "END"
```

Chapter 11: Math

Chapter 11 is about REXX doing what computers were built to do: math.
Computers should compute. All too often the programming language fights with you. You want a decimal, people-friendly number, not some exotic numbering system invented on Mars. Of course, REXX does what you want.

Chapter 11 contains:
    When does REXX do math?   112
    Math: Arithmetic Operators   113
    Math: Precision   114

Chapter 11: Math

Many command procedure languages can't do any kind of arithmetic other than 1 + 1. REXX has a full set of mathematical capabilities. You can do calculations to *any* precision, limited only by the amount of computer resources available.
REXX does its math in decimal numbers at all times, so you won't get an "almost right" answer.

When does REXX do math?
    When there are 2 or more numbers and an arithmetic operator
    not enclosed in quote marks.

Examples:
```
A = 1 + 1
SAY 1 + 1

"SEND 'LUNCH IN " 1 + 1 "HOURS' USER(TSOU02) "
DO I = (0 + 1) TO (100 - 2) /* parens not required here*/
END I
```

Chapter 11: Math

Math: Arithmetic Operators

```
SAY  1 + 1              addition                    --> 2

SAY  2 - 1              subtraction                 --> 1

SAY  2 * 2              multiplication              --> 4

SAY  -1 * 2             multiplication              --> -2

SAY  4 / 2              division                    --> 2

SAY  5 % 2              integer division            --> 2

SAY  5 // 2             remainder                   --> 1

SAY  3 ** 2             exponentiation              --> 9

SAY  (4 + 2) * 3        parentheses to group operations
                                                    --> 18

SAY  4 + (2 * 3)        parentheses to group operations
                                                    --> 10
```

This example shows REXX's arithmetic operators.
    – only % and // are somewhat unusual
    – you have to use the symbols
    – don't use English words such as ADD.

Chapter 11: Math

Math: Precision

If Einstein had had REXX he might have had time to play some golf. REXX does math to whatever precision you desire, limited only by the amount of computer memory you have available. REXX does everything in decimal numbers so you won't see approximate results.

Changing the precision.
The default precision is 9 digits. If a calculation generates more significant digits than that, REXX will round the answer and stop at 9 digits. You can change the precision to 100 or 1000 or 10000! On some systems you can go much higher than that.
Useful for figuring your income tax.....

To change the precision to 100 digits:
```
      NUMERIC DIGITS    100
```
The following example will show you what that means.
```
      /*   REXX Numdig*/
      SAY    2 / 3
      /*displays   .666666667 (9 digits)      */

      NUMERIC DIGITS    100

      SAY 2 / 3

      /*displays
      .6666666666666666666666666666666666
      6666666666666666666666666666666666
      6666666666666666667    */
```

Do Practice Problems 43 – 46.

Chapter 12: Passing Commands to Command Processors

Chapter 12 is about talking to the operating system in which REXX is executing. REXX executes in TSO, ISPF, the ISPF Editor, and other environments.
REXX doesn't do everything! REXX is designed to pass commands to external command processors: operating systems, editors and other programs running in your operating system. The power in your hands is amazing: you can control other programs from inside your REXX program.

Chapter 12 contains:

Passing commands to the environment	116
How Do You Get REXX to Pass a Command to a Command Processor?	117
What Do the Return Codes (RC) mean?	118
What Command Processors Are Out There?	120
How do You Send Commands to a Command Processor?	121
Sending commands to TSO	121
Sending commands to ISPF	122
Sending commands to the ISPF Editor	124
How Does Your Program Know if the Command Processor is There?	126

Chapter 12: Passing Commands to Command Processors

Passing commands to the environment

REXX has the ability to pass commands to an external command processor, sometimes known as the environment. The command processor is an operating system, such as TSO, MVS, VM/CMS, or a program that has the ability to interact with REXX, such as editors, security systems and application development systems.

By default, on TSO, REXX can pass commands to TSO, ISPF, and the ISPF Editor.
On VM/CMS, REXX can pass commands to CMS, CP and XEDIT.

REXX can't syntax check any command that it passes to an external command processor; REXX doesn't attempt to analyze these commands or understand them in any way. It passes them to the external processor, waits for them to end, and captures a return code (the special variable RC) that summarizes how the command worked.

To prevent REXX from trying to analyze a command you must enclose it in double quotes or apostrophes.

Since this is a book about REXX I won't explain operating system commands here. You can get a good summary of TSO commands in my book: *TSO CLIST to TSO REXX: Conversion Handbook*, ISBN-10: 1508668493, ISBN-13: 978-1508668497, available for purchase at online booksellers and where you bought this book.

The next several pages will answer these questions:
- How do you get REXX to pass a command to a command processor?
- What do the return codes (**RC**) mean?
- What command processors are out there?
- How do you send commands to a command processor?
- How does your program know if the command processor is there?

Chapter 12: Passing Commands to Command Processors

How Do You Get REXX to Pass a Command to a Command Processor?

REXX knows its own verbs: **SAY**, **PULL**, **PARSE**, etc. REXX doesn't know or understand TSO or ISPF or any other operating system command. So how does REXX know that it is supposed to pass a command to a command processor?

It will if you use one of the following methods:
(The command is the first thing on the line.)

1. Put the command in double quotes or apostrophes. (Quotes preferred).
```
"LISTCAT"
'LISTDS ABC.DATA'
"SEND 'HELLO THERE WHAT TIME IS LUNCH?' USER(TSOU01)"
```
Double quotes are better on TSO, because some TSO commands use apostrophes, and it avoids conflict.

2. Skip the quotes or apostrophes and hope REXX doesn't choke on the command. (Not good for your sanity).
```
      LISTCAT
```
        no problem for REXX
```
      LISTCAT LEVEL(TSOUID)
```
        REXX gives syntax error (no double quotes or apostrophes)
        looking for built-in function LEVEL
```
      CALL 'SYS1.PGMLIB(PROGRAM1)'    /*(note: no double quotes)*/
```
        REXX thinks this is REXX **CALL** verb
        you thought it was TSO **CALL** command
        REXX gives syntax error.

3. Put the command in parentheses (unusual, but it works).
```
      (LISTCAT)
```

4. Put the command in a variable, then put the variable *first* on the line.
```
      Command = "LISTCAT LEVEL(TSOUID)"    quotes needed here
      Command
```

Chapter 12: Passing Commands to Command Processors

What Do the Return Codes (RC) mean?

Each command sent by REXX to an external command processor sets the special REXX variable **RC** when it finishes. All commands on TSO follow this rule:

RC = 0	command worked correctly
RC > 0	command detected an error
RC = -3	the 'command' does not exist
RC = strange number	you executed a compiled program which terminated abnormally and set a Z/OS System Abend Code. The function D2X(ABS(RC)) shows system abend codes in the traditional Z/OS form, for example 0C7 or 013.

Each command assigns different meanings to return codes. Generally, the higher the number, the worse the error.

Chapter 12: Passing Commands to Command Processors

A few examples:
```
"LISTCAT"     /* COMMAND TO TSO TO LIST DATASETS*/
SAY RC        /* GIVES A 0                      */

"LISTDOG"     /* COMMAND TO TSO THAT IT DOESN'T
                 RECOGNIZE                      */
SAY RC        /* GIVES A -3 'no such command'   */

"%BADDOG"     /* executing another REXX program
                 that returns a high return code on its EXIT
                 statement, like this: EXIT 16 */
SAY RC        /* GIVES A 16  */

"%BADPUP"     /* executing a CLIST
                 that returns a high return code on its EXIT
                 statement, like this: EXIT CODE(16) */
SAY RC        /* GIVES A 16  */
```

> Although you are executing a CLIST or another REXX program, it "looks" like you are executing a TSO command.

Do Practice Problem 47.

Chapter 12: Passing Commands to Command Processors

What Command Processors Are Out There?

A REXX program executing on-line on TSO under z/OS can send commands to the following external command processors:

    TSO.
        TSO commands, such as ALLOCATE and LISTDS.
        Environment name is "TSO"
        `"DELETE 'userid.ABC.DATA'"`

    ISPF.
        display panels
        variable services
        file tailoring
        Environment name is "ISPEXEC"
        `"DISPLAY PANEL(PANL123)"   /* for ISPF */`

    ISPF editor.
        editor macros
        Environment name is "ISREDIT."
        `"(SAVESTAT) = USER_STATE" /*for editor */`

Chapter 12: Passing Commands to Command Processors

How do You Send Commands to a Command Processor?

Sending commands to TSO

No special action is required. TSO is always available when you are logged on to TSO on-line or if you are executing TSO in batch (see Chapter 20) "Running REXX in Batch".

You can send commands to TSO from a REXX program executing in:
- Line Mode ("Ready Mode") TSO
- any ISPF panel.
- TSO in batch (JCL that executes the program IKJEFT1A)

Your program can always talk to TSO. TSO is the default command processor.
Just remember to put your command in double quotes or apostrophes.
Examples:
```
"LISTCAT"
"LISTCAT LEVEL(TSOU01) "
USER = "TSOU01"
"LISTCAT LEVEL("user")"   /* a variable in the TSO
                 command */
"DELETE 'userid.ABC.DATA'"
"LOGOFF"          /*unless you are in ISPF*/
```

In order to send commands to TSO, you never have to say

    ADDRESS TSO

Unless you have previously changed the default ADDRESS environment by means of a

    ADDRESS ISPEXEC or ADDRESS ISREDIT
    On a separate line by itself

Chapter 12: Passing Commands to Command Processors

Sending commands to ISPF

You must be in ISPF! Any ISPF panel will do, including Option 6 – TSO command shell and the ISPF Editor. If you are in Line Mode ("Ready Mode") TSO you can't send commands to ISPF.

You must declare that you want to send commands to ISPF! ISPF is not the default processor (TSO is). Most programmers put **ADDRESS ISPEXEC** in front of the ISPF command:
```
ADDRESS ISPEXEC  "DISPLAY PANEL(PANL123)"
```

ISPEXEC is the official, internal name of ISPF. Your command won't go to ISPF if you don't prefix it with **ADDRESS ISPEXEC** or use one of these alternatives:

1. **ADDRESS ISPEXEC** on a separate line from the ISPF command
```
       ADDRESS ISPEXEC    /*on a separate line!*/
       "command for ISPF here"
       "possibly another command for ISPF here"
       "yet another"
```
   Careful! This sends all subsequent commands to ISPF!
   If you want to send a command to TSO you must now say ADDRESS TSO!

2. Just prefix the command with **ISPEXEC** (no **ADDRESSing**!)
```
       "ISPEXEC DISPLAY PANEL(PANL123)"
```
   ISPEXEC is a TSO command that sends commands to ISPF!
   This will work quite well. It is not the way I do things,
   but I have to show you because many programmers do it.

If you can send commands to ISPF, that implies that you are also in TSO, and that TSO is available to receive commands, if you do the proper **ADDRESSing**.

If you are running ISPF in batch, you can talk to ISPF from a batch job. See my Internet paper at http://TheAmericanProgrammer.com/programming/ispfbatch.shtml

Chapter 12: Passing Commands to Command Processors

Sending commands to ISPF, continued

Here are a few of the things you can do with ISPF commands.

    Storing and retrieving variables
    Displaying panels
    File Tailoring
    Use ISPF tables
    Use Library Management services.

I can't give you the full explanation of using the ISPEXEC environment here, but here are a few examples:

Storing a variable permanently.
```
Name = "John"
ADDRESS ISPEXEC "VPUT (NAME) PROFILE"
```

Storing a variable until you exit from ISPF.
```
Name = "John"
ADDRESS ISPEXEC "VPUT (NAME) "
```

Retrieving a variable you stored
```
ADDRESS ISPEXEC "VGET (NAME)"
Say Name   /* null, if you never stored it */
```

Displaying a panel
```
ADDRESS ISPEXEC "DISPLAY PANEL(panelname)"
```

Chapter 12: Passing Commands to Command Processors

Sending commands to the ISPF Editor (macros)

You must be *in* the ISPF Editor! You must execute your REXX program from the command line of ISPF edit without the word **TSO** in front of the program name.
The absence of "**TSO**" tells the Editor that the program is an ISPF Editor macro.
    Example, in ISPF Edit, on the command line
        `MYPROG        or      %MYPROG`

Executing your program this way is not enough. Your program must start with an **ADDRESS ISREDIT** "**MACRO**" command right after the initial comment. See the example macro shown later in this chapter.

You must show that a command is for the ISPF Editor! Most programmers put **ADDRESS ISREDIT** in front of the ISPF Editor command in their program:
    `ADDRESS ISREDIT "(SAVESTAT) = USER_STATE"`

ISREDIT is the official, internal name of the ISPF Editor. Your command won't go to the editor if you don't prefix it with **ADDRESS ISREDIT** or use one of these alternatives:
1.   **ADDRESS ISREDIT**   on a separate line from the editor command
```
        ADDRESS ISREDIT    /*on a separate line!*/
        "command for editor here"
        "possibly another command for editor here"
        "yet another"
```
    Careful! This sends all subsequent commands to the editor!
    If you want to send a command to TSO you must now say
    ADDRESS TSO; if you want to send a command to ISPF
    you must now say **ADDRESS ISPEXEC**.

2.   Just prefix the command with **ISREDIT** (no **ADDRESS**ing!)
        `"ISREDIT  (SAVESTAT) = USER_STATE"`
    ISREDIT is a TSO command that sends commands to the editor!
    I don't do it this way, but many programmers do.

If you can send commands to the ISPF Editor, **ISREDIT**, that implies that you are also in ISPF (**ISPEXEC**), and that ISPF and TSO are available, so you can also send commands to them if you do the proper **ADDRESS**ing.
See the preceding pages on how to send commands to ISPF and TSO.

Chapter 12: Passing Commands to Command Processors

Sending commands to the ISPF Editor, continued.

What does an edit macro look like? Here is an example of the world's shortest edit macro. It is named SVAE. It does an edit SAVE. You see, my fingers sometimes hit the keys in the wrong order...

```
/*REXX Editor macro SVAE that does a SAVE
*/
   ADDRESS ISREDIT "MACRO"
   ADDRESS ISREDIT "SAVE"
```

A macro must start with the **ADDRESS ISREDIT "MACRO"** or the editor will not let you talk to it. All editor commands will be rejected and your program will fail.
When executing, you must not prefix the program's name with TSO!
If you do, you won't have a macro.

Here is how you would use the SVAE macro shown above in an edit session:

```
EDIT ---'TSOU01.MYPROGS.COBOL(PROG1)'
COMMAND ===>   SVAE                          SCROLL ==> DATA
000100 READ-PARAGRAPH.
000200      READ INPUT-file
000300         AT END MOVE 'Y' TO EOF-SW.
000400
```

If you want to know more about macros, you can pick up my cheat sheet at this web page:
http://TheAmericanProgrammer.com/programming/holymac.shtml

Chapter 12: Passing Commands to Command Processors

How Does Your Program Know if the Command Processor is There?

```
"SUBCOM" "ISPEXEC"
IF RC = 0 THEN DO
      ADDRESS   ISPEXEC   "CONTROL ERRORS RETURN"
      ADDRESS   ISPEXEC   "DISPLAY PANEL(PANEL1)"
            END
ELSE DO
      UID = "TSOU01"
       "SEND 'HELLO THERE  ' USER(" UID ")"
         END
```

You know if a command processor is there. You can see the screen you are on.
REXX can't. However, your REXX program can ask if a command processor is there.
If it isn't there, you had better not try to send commands to it.

Use the **SUBCOM** TSO (and CMS) command. The special variable RC will tell you if that command processor is available, ready to accept your commands.

```
"SUBCOM" "the desired command processor"
```

for example:
```
"SUBCOM" "ISPEXEC" /* ISPF*/
"SUBCOM" "ISREDIT" /* Editor*/
"SUBCOM" "TSO"     /* TSO */
```

Then check **RC**. A zero means that all is well and you can safely send commands to that environment.

Interaction of ADDRESS and "SUBCOM".

You can say **ADDRESS** anything you want, for example **ADDRESS MOON**,
(a command processor that doesn't exist). All subsequent commands will fail.
If you had said **"SUBCOM" "MOON"** first you would have seen that the moon isn't a command processor.

Chapter 13: Built-in Functions

Chapter 13 gives you some of the functions that are included with REXX. Functions are great. They are supplied with the system. You know they work right!

Chapter 13 contains:
    Some examples   128
    Basics of functions   128
    CALLing a function   129
    Some of the more important functions.   130
    Those Conversion Functions   132
    Built-in Functions: TSO Functions   134

Chapter 13: Built-in Functions

Some examples

```
/* REXX Funct*/
SAY LENGTH("ABCDEF")  /*becomes SAY 6, which then displays
                       a "6" at the terminal*/
NAME = "Wilfred"
SAVE_LENGTH = LENGTH(NAME)         /* assignment */

SAY "NAME CONTAINS ",
    LENGTH(NAME) "LETTERS"         /* substitution */

SAY "DOUBLING YOUR NAME'S LENGTH GIVES",
    LENGTH(NAME) * 2 "LETTERS"     /*arith. expression*/
```

Basics of functions

REXX has many useful built-in functions. Functions let you do complex things with simple instructions. This chapter will show you *the more important functions* and the ones that are specific to TSO.

For a description of the functions in REXX see my book *The REXX Language on TSO: **REXX Functions**,* ISBN-10: 1490536078, ISBN-13: 978-1490536071, available for purchase at online booksellers and where you bought this book.

Notice how functions may be used, in the above example. The function invocation is not the first thing on the line, as the vendor manuals imply. It is always used in some instruction. REXX executes the function and substitutes its return value for the function. In the first example above, the LENGTH function asks for the length of ABCDEF. This is 6, which REXX substitutes for the function. It is as if the instruction were: SAY 6.

Note these three points of syntax, when you invoke a function this way:
`SAVE_LENGTH = LENGTH(NAME)`

1. There is no space between the name of the function and the parenthesis.
2. you must separate parameters with commas, not spaces (but extra spaces may be used if desired.)

    ```
    SAY LEFT("ABCD",2)
    /* AB */
    ```

3. the result of the function is not available in variable **RESULT**
    (it is if you use **CALL** – see below.)

Chapter 13: Built-in Functions

```
        /* Rexx Leng*/
        CALL LENGTH "ABCDEF"
        SAY RESULT /* contains a 6, which is displayed */

        CALL LENGTH "ABCDEF"
        SAVE_LENGTH = RESULT      /* assignment */

        NAME = "Wilfred"
        CALL LENGTH NAME
        SAY "NAME CONTAINS ",
            RESULT "LETTERS"      /* substitution*/

        CALL LENGTH NAME
        SAY "DOUBLING YOUR NAME'S LENGTH GIVES",
            RESULT * 2 "LETTERS" /* arithmetic expression */
```

CALLing a function

If you prefer, you may **CALL** any built-in or internal (user-written) function. If you do this, the syntax is slightly different from the normal function invocation shown on the previous page.

This manner of invoking a function is more efficient than the other when you need the result of the function more than once – this allows you to **CALL** the function once and use the result several times in the special variable **RESULT**.

You may want to use this method as well when you really don't want the result at all – as I show you later with the function **MSG**.

Note these points of syntax for **CALLing** a function
- There is no parenthesis between the name of the function and the parameters.
- The function always returns a value on its **RETURN** statement.
    It appears in the reserved variable **RESULT**.
    The value will sometimes be zero characters or null!
- you must separate parameters with commas, not spaces (but extra spaces may be used if desired.)

```
CALL LEFT "ABCD",2
SAY RESULT
/* AB */
```

Chapter 13: Built-in Functions

Some of the more important functions.

DATATYPE   checks numbers for validity
```
    SAY DATATYPE(123)   /*--> NUM  */
    SAY DATATYPE(ABCD)  /*--> CHAR */
```

LENGTH   gives the number of characters in a string.
```
    SAY LENGTH("ABCD") /*--> 4*/

    NAME = "Sue Ann"
    SAY LENGTH(NAME)   /*--> 7*/
```

FORMAT   gives the desired number of digit positions
```
    SAY FORMAT(input-number, positions-before, positions-after)
```
       input-number is a number or variable containing a number
       positions-before is how many whole number positions desired
       positions-after is how many positions desired after the decimal point

```
    SAY FORMAT(100.4,3,2)   /*--> 100.40  */

    number = 100.6
    SAY FORMAT(number,4,3) /*--> 100.600 */
                     (space before 100)

    number = 100000.6
    SAY FORMAT(number,4,3)   /*-->  REXX syntax error
                because significant digits would be lost*/
```

POS   is a character string present?
```
    SAY POS(needle, haystack)

    SAY POS("C","ABCDEF") /*--> 3*/
    SAY POS("X","ABCDEF") /*--> 0*/
```

Chapter 13: Built-in Functions

QUEUED()   number of lines currently available in the Internal Data Queue (Stack).

```
PUSH "ABCDEF"
SAY QUEUED() /*--> 1 */

/* write to a file from the Stack */
"EXECIO " QUEUED()" DISKW OUTFILE (FINIS) "
    /* (See Chapter 18 on File IO)*/
DO QUEUED()    /*clean out the Stack */
PULL .
END
```

SUBSTR   returns a portion of a *string*
                        beginning at *start-pos*, for *length*. */

```
SAY SUBSTR(string, start-pos, length)

SAY SUBSTR("ABCDEF",3,2) /*--> CD */
```

TRANSLATE

    converts characters in *string*
    changes any occurrence of character 1 in input table
    to character 1 of output table; character 2 to character 2, and so on

```
NEW_STRING = TRANSLATE(string, output-table, input-table)

/* note that there is a space after NOYEM */
NEW_STRING = TRANSLATE("DINERO", "NOYEM ","NIREDO")
SAY NEW_STRING /* produces 'MONEY' */
```

You can use TRANSLATE to change to upper case
```
UPPER_STRING = TRANSLATE(LOWER_CASE_STRING)
```

This is an interesting feature of TRANSLATE.
It will change the order of characters in a string.
```
SAY TRANSLATE("123456789","ABCDEFGHI","123456798")
    /* produces ABCDEFGIH */
```

Chapter 13: Built-in Functions

Those Conversion Functions
It isn't always clear from the vendor manuals how the character conversion functions work. A problem arises from the use of the word "HEX". I use HEX below to refer to a number that is in the hexadecimal numbering system, based on 16 rather than on 10.

I use "EBCDIC Internal Representation" to mean the way a character is represented in the computer's memory. The manuals sometimes refer to this as HEX. It isn't HEX. EBCDIC refers to a conversion scheme that is used on IBM mainframe computers.
It is contrasted with ASCII which is used on most other computers.

Please inspect the following examples of conversion functions. Note that you will get different results on an ASCII computer.

Chapter 13: Built-in Functions

Examples of conversion functions

C2D
first converts character to EBCDIC internal representation (C1)
then converts that to a decimal number   (193)
```
SAY C2D("A") /* "193" */
```
another example:
```
SAY C2D("1") /* "241"  */
```

C2X
A in EBCDIC internal representation is C1
```
SAY C2X("A") /* "C1" */
```
another example:
```
SAY C2X("1") /* "F1" */
```

D2C
this is the converse of C2D
```
SAY D2C(193) /* "A" */
SAY D2C(241) /* "1" */
```

D2X
Converts decimal number to hex
```
SAY D2X(15) /* "F" */
```
another example:
```
SAY D2X(16) /* "10" */
```

X2C
converts EBCDIC internal representation to character
```
SAY X2C(F1) /* "1" */
```

X2D
converts hex number to decimal
```
SAY X2D(0F) /* "15" */
SAY X2D(10) /* "16" */
```

Chapter 13: Built-in Functions

Built-in Functions: TSO Functions
Some functions are found only on TSO. They interact with operating system services that are found only in TSO.

LISTDSI TSO Only.

      RET_CODE = LISTDSI(*dataset name* NORECALL)
        or
      CALL LISTDSI *dataset name* NORECALL
      RET_CODE = RESULT

Retrieves information about *dataset name* and puts it into variables:
The more important variables are:
SYSDSORG   PS: sequential   PO: partitioned
                         DA: direct   VS: VSAM
SYSRECFM   F: fixed   V: variable   B: blocked
                         A: ASA printer control
SYSLRECL   Logical record length
SYSBLKSIZE   Block size

A Return code of 0 indicates that it worked correctly.
A Return code of 4 usually means that the dataset had been migrated,
      you specified NORECALL and so some information is missing.
A Return code of 16 indicates that it did not work correctly
        – examine the variable SYSREASON (see IBM manual)

Optional NORECALL keyword prevents a recall of the dataset if it has been migrated.
Then the function will not return complete information.
Optional DIRECTORY keyword retrieves PDS information,
      Such as number of members in the variable SYSMEMBERS
Optional SMSINFO keyword retrieves SMS information,
      Such as storage class in the variable SYSSTORCLASS.

Examples:
```
    DSN = "'userid.MY.REXX.EXEC'"
    Call LISTDSI    DSN    NORECALL
    Say    SYSDSORG    SYSRECFM    SYSLRECL    SYSBLKSIZE

    /* Also:*/
    DSN = "'userid.MY.REXX.EXEC'"
    Ret_code = LISTDSI(DSN    NORECALL)
    Say    SYSDSORG    SYSRECFM    SYSLRECL    SYSBLKSIZE
```

Chapter 13: Built-in Functions

MSG Function (TSO Only)

SAY MSG()   Returns the current setting of MSG, whether or not TSO command error messages are displayed. Returns either ON (the default) or OFF.
    Example:

```
SAY MSG()  /* ON */
-or-
/* when you don't need to see current setting: */
CALL MSG "OFF"
-or-
X = MSG("OFF")
```

MESSAGE_SETTING = MSG("ON")
or
MESSAGE_SETTING = MSG("OFF")
    Returns the current setting of MSG: ON if TSO command error messages are displayed and OFF if not.
    A value in the parentheses changes the setting to that value.
    A setting of "OFF" hides error messages from TSO commands, as when deleting a file that doesn't exist.

    Example:

```
MESSAGE_SETTING = MSG("OFF")   /*value was on.
                                 turn it off */
SAY MSG()                      /*displays OFF*/

SAY MESSAGE_SETTING            /*displays ON */
```

Note that MSG "OFF" hides error messages from system commands. It does not hide normal displayed output from these commands.
This is useful when you don't want to confuse the user with TSO's error messages.
The command still doesn't work, but the user is unaware.

Chapter 13: Built-in Functions

OUTTRAP Function (TSO Only)

CALL OUTTRAP *"stem.", "how-many-lines"*   Turns on capturing of the display output of TSO commands, such as "LISTCAT," "LISTDS," error messages as from "DELETE file-that-doesn't-exist" SAY in another EXEC, or a WRITE in a CLIST.
Each line of output is captured in a different element of the array created from *stem*.
A maximum of *how-many-lines* will be captured, with "*" meaning "capture all lines."

    Returns:

    stem.0 contains the line number of the last line
           (I.E. how many lines returned)
    stem.1 contains the first line
    stem.2 contains the second line, etc.
    stem.n contains the last line, etc.

Example:

```
CALL OUTTRAP "LINE.", "*"
"LISTDS NO.SUCH.DATASET"
SAY LINE.1/* Display first line:
          DATASET NO.SUCH.DATASET NOT IN CATALOG */
SAY LINE.0/* How many lines (1)*/

DO I = 1 to LINE.0 /* this loop displays all lines */
    Say Line.I
END I
```

CALL OUTTRAP "OFF"   Turns off the trapping of command output so the commands will resume displaying their output at the terminal.

CALL OUTTRAP "LINE.", "0"   Discards the displayed output of commands such as "LISTCAT," "LISTDS," error messages as from "DELETE DOESNT.EXIST," SAY in another EXEC, or a WRITE in a CLIST.
The output is not displayed at the terminal and is not captured.

Chapter 13: Built-in Functions

SYSDSN TSO Only.

SAY SYSDSN(*dataset name*)

Tells if *dataset name* exists, or what its status is.

Returns:

```
OK              (dataset name exists as specified)
MEMBER SPECIFIED BUT DATASET NOT PDS
MEMBER NOT FOUND
DATASET NOT FOUND
ERROR PROCESSING REQUESTED DATASET
PROTECTED DATASET
VOLUME NOT ON SYSTEM
UNAVAILABLE DATASET
INVALID DATASET NAME
MISSING DATASET NAME
```

Examples:

```
IF SYSDSN("'userid.JCL.CNTL(JOB001)'") = "OK"
THEN
   DO
     "SUBMIT 'userid.JCL.CNTL(JOB001)'"
   END
ELSE
   DO
     SAY SYSDSN("'userid.JCL.CNTL(JOB001)'")
   END
```

Do Practice Problems 48 – 54

Chapter 14: Writing Your Own Functions

Chapter 14 shows you how to create useful functions to simplify your programming.
REXX believes in sharing the wealth. You can create your own functions that are as robust, consistent and useful as the built-in ones.

Chapter 14 contains:
    Example of Internal Function   140
    Internal, user-written functions   140
    What makes a function a function?   142
    Protecting Variables   143
    Example of External Function   144
    External, user-written functions   144
    Search Order for Functions and Subroutines   145

Chapter 14: Writing Your Own Functions

Example of Internal Function
The numbers are explained on the next page.

```
        /* REXX sample program*/
 [1]   Say Sayhello("Mary") /*the invoking instruction*/

 [2]   Call Sayhello "Mary" /*the invoking instruction*/
        Say result
                        [3]
        Exit
 [4]
        Sayhello:
                      [5]
        ARG INPUT

        OUTPUT = "HELLO" INPUT
        Return OUTPUT            [6]
```

Internal, user-written functions
You can create your own functions that act like the built-in ones. You may use functions for convenience, to simplify your programming, and to achieve uniformity by using the same function over and over again in many programs.

A function is a section of REXX code that performs a useful action. A function may be internal – contained inside the program that uses it, or external – contained in a separate member in your REXX PDS. This chapter will show you an internal function first, then an external function.

Chapter 14: Writing Your Own Functions

Description of the example on the previous page
Referring to the numbers in the boxes:

1. one way of invoking a function (the more common way)
   - if you do it this way, the answer from the function replaces the invocation.
   - it is as if you said **SAY HELLO Mary**

2. another way of invoking the function (**CALL**)
   - if you do it this way, your answer is found in the special variable **RESULT**

3. please put your functions at the physical end of your program
   - and put an **EXIT** before them, so control won't fall into the functions

4. the internal function actually is the code after the label
   - **Sayhello:**
   - through the **RETURN**

5. a properly-written internal user-written function receives its input on an ARG statement. You pass the information on the same line as the CALL instruction.

> Please separate the ARG variables with commas:
> ```
> Myfunc:
> Arg var1, var2, var3, etc
> ```
> Also separate the data items passed to the function with commas
> ```
> x = Myfunc("abc", "def", "ghi", etc)
> ```

6. a function *must* return something on its RETURN statement
   - or it's not a function
   - this answer may be a number,
     - one or more character strings,   "HELLO" "GOODBYE"
     - a variable,   NAME
     - or the null string   ""
     - Do not use commas to separate character strings.

Chapter 14: Writing Your Own Functions

```
/* REXX sample program containing an internal
function*/
Say Doublit(4) /*the invoking instruction*/

Call Doublit "4" /*the invoking instruction*/
Say result

Exit


Doublit:
ARG INPUT_NUMBER
/* do some processing */
Return INPUT_NUMBER * 2
```

Executing the function

The function

What makes a function a function?
A function has an **ARG** and a **RETURN**.

The function receives the argument(s) by means of its **ARG** or **PARSE ARG** statement.
It performs some processing and gives back a computed answer on its **RETURN** statement. This answer may be a number, one or character strings, or the null string, *but it must be there*.

A function receives one or more parameters (arguments) passed to it when it is invoked.
`Say Myfunc("abcd") /*the invoking instruction*/`

`Call Myfunc "abcd" /*the invoking instruction*`
`Say result`

The parameters may be a null string – zero characters.
`Say Myfunc("") /*the invoking instruction*/`

`Call Myfunc "" /*the invoking instruction*/`
`Say result`

Do Practice Problem 55.

Chapter 14: Writing Your Own Functions

Protecting Variables

By default, all variables in an internal, user-written function (and subroutine as well) are shared with the main part of the program.

To protect variables from sharing use the **PROCEDURE** instruction in an internal function.
Example:
```
Myfunc: PROCEDURE
ARG INPUT

Return "xyz"
```
INPUT will be protected. Any change you make to it in the function will not be reflected in the main part of the program, and vice versa.

Sharing variables, again

If you want to protect most variables but share some, use the **PROCEDURE** instruction with the **EXPOSE** option in an internal function.
Example:
```
Myfunc: PROCEDURE EXPOSE INPUT
ARG INPUT

Return "xyz"
```
Input will be shared once again. If you want to share two or more variables, list them one after another:
`PROCEDURE EXPOSE VAR1 VAR2...`
All other variables will be protected (not shared).

Chapter 14: Writing Your Own Functions

Example of External Function

```
/* REXX sample program*/
Say Sayhello("Mary")  /*the invoking instruction*/

Call Sayhello "Mary"  /*the invoking instruction*/
Say result

Exit

----------------------------------------------------
            /* REXX Sayhello. Not in this member*/

            ARG INPUT

            OUTPUT = "HELLO"INPUT
            Return OUTPUT
```

External, user-written functions
Please note the following characteristics of an external, user-written function:

- is a separate member in the same PDS the main program is in
- or is a member in a PDS assigned with the **ALTLIB** command
- or is a member in a PDS concatenated to **SYSEXEC/SYSPROC**
- its name must be 8 characters or less, begin with a letter, and contain letters or numbers
- there is no **PROCEDURE** statement (it causes a syntax error)
- a label is not used to define the external function/subroutine
- you must pass information through an **ARG**

commas should be used to separate the items on the **ARG**.
note: you may pass a maximum of 20 items

- you must send information back to the caller through a **RETURN**

Do not use commas to separate character strings in the information on the **RETURN**.

An external, user-written function works just like an internal one. You would create an external function because you want other users to be able to use it. There is a slight performance penalty for using external instead of internal.

Chapter 14: Writing Your Own Functions

Search Order for Functions and Subroutines (TSO only)

The functions that you write may be internal or external.
If external, they may be on any PDS that TSO can access.

The PDS may be assigned to **SYSEXEC** or **SYSPROC**, or you may have used the **TSO ALTLIB** command (see Chapter 2) to tell TSO to access the PDS.

The table just below tells you the order in which TSO will search these PDSs. The first time that a member name is found, the search stops.

The strike-out (~~Internal, user-written~~) is used to show that that one is not searched).

Double quotes or apostrophes	**No quotes around name**
SAY "MYFUNC"(parameters)	SAY MYFUNC(parameters)
~~Internal, user-written~~	Internal, user-written
Built-in	Built-in
External, same PDS	External, same PDS
External, PDS assigned by ALTLIB	External, PDS assigned by ALTLIB
External, PDS assigned to SYSEXEC	External, PDS assigned to SYSEXEC
External, PDS assigned to SYSPROC	External, PDS assigned to SYSPROC

Please notice in the above table that quotes around a function name may be used to make TSO ignore any internal function, and to look for built-in or external ones (by the same name) instead.

Chapter 15: Writing Your Own Subroutines

Chapter 15 is about creating your own subroutines.
A subroutine is not the same as a function. Subroutines are not subject to as many rules as functions. Using them can simplify the logic of your program. A tangled mess of logic is an unreliable program that is going to break sometime soon.

Chapter 15 contains:
    Example   148
    Writing internal subroutines   148

Chapter 15: Writing Your Own Subroutines

Example

```
/* REXX */
/* instructions */
NUM1 = 5
NUM2 = 6
CALL MYSUB       /* executing the sub */
/* instructions */
/* instructions */
EXIT

MYSUB: /* the subroutine */
ANSWER = NUM1 + NUM2
SAY ANSWER
RETURN
```

Writing internal subroutines

An internal subroutine is used to simplify coding – to avoid long cumbersome logic structures.

A subroutine has some things in common with a function, but it's not a function.
Here are the characteristics of a subroutine:

- Invoked by: `CALL subroutine-name`
- Example: `CALL ADDEM`
- **ARG** is optional
- You don't have to pass information to your subroutine on the same line as the `CALL` instruction.
- **RETURN** is required but you don't have to pass information back on it
  If you do, the information is available in the **RESULT** variable
- Variables are shared with the main part of the program
- Using the **PROCEDURE** instruction is not required, since it hides all the variables in the subroutine from the main part of the program
- There are no external subroutines.

Do Practice Problems 56 – 61.

Chapter 16: The Internal Data Queue, or Stack

Chapter 16 is about a feature of REXX that you will either love or hate.
It's either a convenience or a confusing feature. It depends on your point of view.
I don't believe that you should go out of your way to use the Internal Data Queue in every program, but it can be a useful place to put things you'll need later.
But watch out if you leave things dangling in it when you end your program.

Chapter 16 contains:
What is it?	150
How do you put things into the Internal Data Queue	150
Internal Data Queue or terminal dialogue?	151
Functions used with the Internal Data Queue	152
Leftovers	153
Clean up after yourself	153

Chapter 16: The Internal Data Queue, or Stack

What is it?
REXX provides a temporary, buffer-like storage area in memory. REXX will obtain as much volatile storage as it can to hold what you put into it. If it can't obtain enough, your program will crash.

Important points to note about the Internal Data Queue:
- created when you first start a REXX program
- any REXX program it calls can use the Internal Data Queue
- the Internal Data Queue is deleted when the all REXX programs have ended
    but see the warning about leaving thing in the Internal Data Queue
    (see the Topic 'leftovers' several pages below)
- CLIST's don't have access to the Internal Data Queue

How do you put things into the Internal Data Queue?
- reading files with **EXECIO (FIFO)**
    Example: `"EXECIO * DISKR INFILE"`

- **QUEUE (FIFO)**
    Example: `QUEUE "Mary"`

- **PUSH (LIFO)**
    Example: `PUSH "CART"`

How do you take things from the Internal Data Queue (Stack)?
- **PULL**
    Example: `PULL NAME`
                        `SAY NAME`

- writing files with EXECIO
    Example: `"EXECIO 1 DISKW OUTFILE"`

- with some TSO commands that have subcommands, such as Line Mode Edit.

Chapter 16: The Internal Data Queue, or Stack

```
PUSH "CLARABELLE"         /*something is in stack now! */

SAY "PLEASE ENTER YOUR NAME"  /* go ahead, type it in*/

PULL NAME                 /* where does it PULL it from? */

SAY "THANK YOU " NAME     /* what does it display?*/
```

Internal Data Queue or terminal dialogue?
Wait a minute – I thought that **SAY** and **PULL** were used to communicate with the user at the terminal? They are. When you do a **SAY "ENTER SOMETHING"** followed by a **PULL** variable, you are doing terminal dialogue.

The problem is that **PULL** goes looking in the Internal Data Queue before it goes to the terminal. So if you have data in the Internal Data Queue you can't do **SAY** and **PULL** for terminal dialogue. Try the above example. What name does it display?

How do I get around that? Two ways:

1. Isolate the existing Internal Data Queue
    Example:
    ```
    "NEWSTACK" /* create a new Stack */
    SAY "PLEASE ENTER YOUR NAME"
    PULL NAME
    "DELSTACK" /* delete the new Stack */
    ```

Use **NEWSTACK** and **DELSTACK** anytime you don't want to disturb the contents of the Internal Data Queue.

2. Use **PARSE EXTERNAL variable** instead of **PULL**
    Example:
    ```
    SAY "PLEASE ENTER YOUR NAME"
    PARSE EXTERNAL NAME
    ```

Chapter 16: The Internal Data Queue, or Stack

Functions used with the Internal Data Queue

QSTACK – how many Internal Data Queues (Stacks).were created by **NEWSTACK**?
   subtract one from RC to find out
   Example:
```
 "QSTACK"
 NUM_BUFFS = RC - 1
 SAY "THERE ARE " NUM_BUFFS " NEW STACKS " /* 0 */
"NEWSTACK"
 "QSTACK"
 NUM_BUFFS = RC - 1
 SAY "THERE ARE " NUM_BUFFS " NEW STACKS " /* 1 */
 "DELSTACK" /*do 1 DELSTACK for every NEWSTACK
                           that you did */
```

QUEUED() – how many lines are available in the currently-active Internal Data Queue (Stack)? or how many PULLs you have to do to empty it?.
   Example:
```
SAY QUEUED()    /* will be zero*/
QUEUE "HELLO"
SAY QUEUED()    /* 1 */
PULL GREETING
SAY GREETING    /* HELLO */
SAY QUEUED()    /* will be zero*/

/*Cleaning out the Internal Data Queue (Stack):*/
DO QUEUED()
      PULL
END
```

Chapter 16: The Internal Data Queue, or Stack

```
PUSH "CLARABELLE"          /*something is in Stack now! */

PUSH "BOZO"                /*two things in Stack now!   */

PULL NAME                  /* take ONE thing from Stack */

SAY "THANK YOU " NAME "FOR CLOWNING AROUND"
```

Leftovers
You really don't want to leave anything in the Internal Data Queue when your program finishes. The above example puts two things into the Internal Data Queue but takes only one out.
Here's what happens:
The remaining line in the Internal Data Queue (Clarabelle) looks just like something you typed in at the terminal, so TSO thinks it's a TSO command and tries to execute it. Put the code shown just below in your program, just before its EXIT and in its HALT trap (See Chapter 9)

Clean up after yourself.
If you used **NEWSTACK** this code will clear everything from *all* Internal Data Queues:

```
"QSTACK"
How_many = RC
Do How_many
   "DELSTACK"
END
```

If you didn't use **NEWSTACK** this code will clear everything from the Internal Data Queue:

```
DO QUEUED()
    Pull
END
```

If you put the previous code segment together with the clown example at the top of the page, you will not see the error message from TSO.

```
PUSH "CLARABELLE"          /*something is in Stack now! */

PUSH "BOZO"                /*two things in Stack now!   */

PULL NAME                  /* take ONE thing from Stack */

SAY "THANK YOU " NAME "FOR CLOWNING AROUND"

DO QUEUED()
    Pull
END
```

Chapter 17: Compound Variables

Chapter 17 shows you a feature of REXX that is something like subscripted variables, but much more powerful. Compound Variables make reading and writing files much easier. They provide a rapid way to look up information stored in memory.

Chapter 17 contains:
    Compared to traditional subscripted variables   156
    Understanding Compound Variables   157
    Examples   158

Chapter 17: Compound Variables

```
Traditional subscripted variables vs REXX compound variables

Traditional (BASIC)          REXX

DAY(1) = "MON"               DAY.1 = "MON"
DAY(2) = "TUE"               DAY.2 = "TUE"
DAY(3) = "WED"               DAY.3 = "WED"
DAY(4) = "THU"               DAY.4 = "THU"

FOR I = 1 TO 4               DO I = 1 TO 4
   PRINT DAY(I)                 SAY DAY.I
NEXT I                       END I
```

REXX Compound Variables do everything that subscripted variables do in traditional programming languages. They allow you to define one data item: the array (DAY, above), and to create and use multiple occurrences, or clones, of it.

But there are differences. REXX Compound Variables are unlike subscripted variables in these ways:
- You don't have to define anything. You just start using them.
- No parenthesis is used. Instead you use a period before the subscript.
- The subscript in REXX doesn't have to be a number. Any character string will work as a subscript.
- The "subscript" is actually called an extension.

Example:
```
      Phone.JANE = "4123212"
      I = "JANE"
      Say Phone.I
/*Well, so what! Why is that good? Watch. This is a continuation of the previous.*/
      Name = "JANE"
      Say Phone.Name /* gives 4123212 */
/*Even better. This is a continuation of the previous two:*/
      Say "Enter a name"
      Pull Name      /* type in JANE */
      say Phone.Name/* gives 4123212 */
```

Chapter 17: Compound Variables

```
WEEKDAY.1 = "MONDAY"
A = 1
SAY WEEKDAY.A
```

Understanding Compound Variables
A REXX compound variable is a two part variable, consisting of:
> the stem
> and
> the extension

with a period in between. In the above example, `WEEKDAY` is the stem. 1 is the extension on the line `WEEKDAY.1 = "MONDAY"`
`A` is the extension on the line `SAY WEEKDAY.A`

Here's how REXX processes the line `WEEKDAY.1 = "MONDAY"`
1. It examines the extension 1.
2. It sees that 1 is not a variable, but a literal.
3. It treats `WEEKDAY.1` as a variable and sets it to `MONDAY`.

Here's how REXX processes the line `SAY WEEKDAY.A` Note that A was set to 1.
1. REXX examines `WEEKDAY.A`.
2. It checks to see if A is a variable; it is, so it must do number 3, next:
3. It retrieves the value of A, which is 1.
4. REXX now examines the complete variable `WEEKDAY.1`
5. `WEEKDAY.1` is now the only variable in the instruction.
6. It looks to see if `WEEKDAY.1` is a variable; it is.
7. It retrieves the value of `WEEKDAY.1`, which is `MONDAY`.

To summarize: REXX looks at the extension first. Is it a variable?
Yes – get its value and put it there: that's the full name of the variable.
No – go no further: that's the full name of the variable.

Chapter 17: Compound Variables

Examples:
This example shows how a compound variable can use a person's name as a "subscript".
```
Student = "JOE"
Grade.Student = 98.2
Student = "CURLY"
Grade.Student = 89
Student = "MOE"
Grade.Student = 77
Say "Whose grade do you want? (Joe, Curly, Moe)"
Pull Who
Say "The grade for " Who " is " Grade.Who
```

This example goes even further, and shows how you can have a kind of random access memory.
```
    DO 10 /*ask names and ages*/
       SAY "WHAT IS YOUR NAME? ('END' TO STOP) "
       PULL NAME
       IF NAME = "END" THEN LEAVE
       SAY "THANK YOU, " NAME ", HOW OLD ARE YOU?"
       PULL HOW_OLD
      AGE.NAME = HOW_OLD
    END /*ASK NAMES */

    /* NOW ALLOW PERSON TO INQUIRE */
    DO 10 /*RETRIEVE AGES*/
       SAY "WHOSE AGE DO YOU WANT TO KNOW?" ,
           " ('END' TO STOP)"
       PULL NAME
       IF NAME = "END" THEN LEAVE
       IF SYMBOL('AGE.NAME') <> "VAR"
       THEN  SAY "THAT NAME NOT NOW IN MEMORY"
       ELSE  SAY NAME " IS " AGE.NAME " OLD "
    END /*RETRIEVE AGES*/
```

Chapter 17: Compound Variables

Examples:
EXECIO lets you use the Internal Data Queue or Compound Variables to hold data being read or written. See the example in Chapter 18 on EXECIO.

The **OUTTRAP** function uses Compound Variables. OUTTRAP allows you to execute a TSO command in your program and capture the command's displayed messages in your program.
```
CALL OUTTRAP "LINE.","*"
"LISTCAT"
DO I = 1 TO LINE.0
   SAY LINE.I
END
```
This function sets Compound Variables.
LINE. tells REXX to set one or more Compound Variables built on this stem. LINE.1 is set to the first line displayed.
Line.2 is set to the second line.
Line.n is set to the last line displayed.
LINE.0 is set to a number that tells you how many lines were displayed.

Changing the stem
If you change the stem, you change all the elements, all the individual variables.
```
WEEKDAY. = "UNKNOWN"
```
Sets WEEKDAY.1, WEEKDAY.1000000000, WEEKDAY.YADAYADA to UNKNOWN.

In addition, it establishes a default value, so that if you try to get the value of something you never set, you get the default.
```
WEEKDAY.      =          "UNKNOWN"
SAY WEEKDAY.99           /*UNKNOWN*/
WEEKDAY.1     =          "SUNDAY"
SAY WEEKDAY.1            /*SUNDAY*/
SAY WEEKDAY.98           /*UNKNOWN*/
SAY WEEKDAY.BLABLA       /* UNKNOWN */
```

To **undefine** all the variables built on a stem (and to reclaim the memory being used) you may:
```
DROP WEEKDAY. /* that's WEEKDAY period */
```

Chapter 17: Compound Variables

Examples:

You can use two or more extensions in order to obtain a multidimensional array. This is a good example, but it will take you about 23 hours and 42 minutes to run.

```
DO DAY = 1 TO 7
   DO HOUR = 1 TO 24
      DO CHANNEL = 2 TO 70
          SAY "PLEASE ENTER THE NAME OF"
          SAY "THE TV PROGRAM"
          SAY "FOR DAY:" DAY
          SAY "FOR HOUR:" HOUR
          SAY "FOR CHANNEL:" CHANNEL
          PULL PROG.DAY.HOUR.CHANNEL
      END CHANNEL
   END HOUR
END DAY

SAY "WHICH DAY'S PROGRAMMING WOULD ",
    "YOU LIKE TO ASK ABOUT?"
PULL DAY
SAY "WHICH HOUR'S PROGRAMMING WOULD ",
    "YOU LIKE TO ASK ABOUT?"
PULL HOUR
SAY "WHICH CHANNEL'S PROGRAMMING WOULD ",
    "YOU LIKE TO ASK ABOUT?"
PULL CHANNEL

SAY "THE PROGRAM THAT IS ON AT THAT TIME"
SAY "IS: " PROG.DAY.HOUR.CHANNEL
```

Do Practice Problems 62 – 63.

Chapter 18: Reading and Writing Files: EXECIO

Chapter 18 shows you that REXX is a full-function programming language. It can process data in external files.
REXX under TSO (and CMS) use EXECIO to read and write files. You can use the simplest of file structures: ordinary sequential files or PDS members (TSO only). Features such as indexed files and data bases are not available in REXX "out of the box".

Chapter 18 contains:

The Basics	162
The ALLOCATE command for reading	163
Reading with EXECIO	164
Reading whole file with EXECIO into Internal Data Queue – example	165
Reading one record at a time into Internal Data Queue – example	166
Reading whole file with EXECIO into an array – example	167
Additional options for Reading	168
The ALLOCATE command for writing	169
Writing with EXECIO	170
Writing whole file from Internal Data Queue – example	171
Writing whole file from an array – example	172

Chapter 18: Reading and Writing Files: EXECIO

The Basics.
EXECIO is found in TSO and VM/CMS REXX. You can read and write sequential files and library (PDS) members.

EXECIO follows the same rules that other input-output methods follow on TSO. This means that you have to follow this sequence of events:

- A `TSO ALLOCATE` command must be done first. It establishes a connection between a pointer to the file (a "DDNAME") and the actual file.
- If running REXX in batch, a JCL DD statement may be done instead.
- The **EXECIO** command is done. This opens and reads or writes the file.
- Close the file. This is done with an **EXECIO** command with the `FINIS` option.
- De-allocate the file with the `TSO FREE` command.
  This breaks the connection between the file and the pointer (the "DDNAME")

EXECIO is executed like a TSO command: it must be in double quotes or apostrophes. It gives a return code in the special variable RC to tell you how it worked.
Here are the values of RC:
     0 = OK
     1 = truncation on writing
     2 = end of file on reading
     20 = serious error

Chapter 18: Reading and Writing Files: EXECIO

The ALLOCATE command for reading.
If the **ALLOCATE** command doesn't work, your **EXECIO** will fail with numerous error messages. First, let's look at the **ALLOCATE** command used with reading.

```
"ALLOC DDN(ddname) SHR REUSE" "DSN('file-you-are-reading')"
```

Explanation of this command.
- **ALLOC** is the abbreviation of **ALLOCATE**.
- **DDN** is the abbreviation of **DDNAME**. This is equivalent to a JCL DD statement.
    An alternate form is **F(ddname)** or **FILE(ddname)**.
    I suggest you use **DDN**, since this corresponds to the JCL parameter **DDNAME**.

- Big trouble if you use a **DDNAME** that TSO is already using for some other purpose. Use a name that doesn't start with **SYS**.
- **SHR** means that you don't mind if other users or jobs read this file at the same time as you.
- **REUSE** means that you will reassign or reuse this file pointer (DDNAME) if you have already used it since logging on to TSO. If not, no harm done.
- **DSN** is the actual file name or dataset name you are trying to read. It must exist. You may also specify a PDS with member name in this form: **MYLIB(MEMBER)**
    An alternate form is **DA('file-name-you-are-reading')**
    I suggest you use **DSN**, since this corresponds to the JCL parameter **DSNAME**.

You may want to check the return code (**RC**) from the **ALLOC** command. If it is not zero, your **EXECIO** will fail with numerous error messages.

Chapter 18: Reading and Writing Files: EXECIO

Reading with EXECIO
You can read:
- the entire file all at once (if there's enough memory available)
- one record at a time
- a specific number of records at a time.

You can read into
- the Internal Data Queue (FIFO)
- Compound Variables

Here is a generic form of the command for reading: (examples follow)
`"EXECIO how-many  DISKR ddname   seq (options)"`

Note these points:
- *How-many* is the number of records that are to be read or written.
    It may not be omitted.
    * may be used to read the whole file (not used for writing)

- `DISKR` means "Disk Read"

- *ddname* is the `DDNAME` you used in the `ALLOC` command

- *Seq* stands for the sequence number of the desired record, but note:
    – It is generally omitted.
    – It allows you to skip records on a read.
    – It does not allow you to jump backwards in the file.
    – You may not use it on a write.

- *Options* there are a few options of interest:
    – If all options are omitted it means that the Internal Data Queue will be used.
    – If `STEM` is specified, it means that an array formed with a compound
        variable will be used.
    – `FINIS` if you wish to close a file at the finish of the read or write
        operation, you may specify the option `FINIS`.
        Please do not omit the closing parenthesis.

Chapter 18: Reading and Writing Files: EXECIO

```
"NEWSTACK"
"ALLOC DDN(INFILE) SHR REUSE DSN('userid.ABC.DATA')"
"EXECIO * DISKR INFILE (FINIS)"

 DO QUEUED()
   PULL RECORD
   SAY RECORD
 END

"DELSTACK"
"FREE DDN(INFILE)"
```

Reading whole file with EXECIO into the Internal Data Queue – example
The above example will read and display all records of a file named **ABC.DATA** into the Internal Data Queue. Here is an explanation of the program.
- **NEWSTACK** Protects the contents of the Internal Data Queue.
  omit if nothing is in Internal Data Queue
- **ALLOC** assigns the file pointer name **INFILE** to the file **ABC.DATA**
- **EXECIO** with the **FINIS** option opens, reads the file and closes it. "*" means "read the whole file".
- **DO QUEUED()** starts a loop that repeats as many times as there are lines in the Internal Data Queue.
- **PULL RECORD** removes a record from the Internal Data Queue and puts it into the variable **RECORD**
- **SAY RECORD** displays the record
- **END** ends the loop
- **DELSTACK** deletes the new Internal Data Queue created by **NEWSTACK**.
- **FREE** reverses the action of the **ALLOC**

Why **FINIS**?
FINIS closes the file. If you don't close, you can't **FREE**.

Why **FREE**?
FREEing a file allows other users or jobs to access it any way they wish. Otherwise allocation remains in effect until you logoff TSO.
There is no reason to omit the close-parenthesis after **FINIS**.

Chapter 18: Reading and Writing Files: EXECIO

```
"NEWSTACK"
"ALLOC DDN(INFILE) SHR REUSE DSN('userid.INPUT.DATA')"

EOF = "NO"
Call Readit

DO I = 1 WHILE EOF = "NO"
   SAY "RECORD NUMBER " I " WAS READ "
   PULL RECORD
   SAY RECORD
   Call Readit
END

"DELSTACK"
"EXECIO 0 DISKR INFILE (FINIS)" /*CLOSE THE FILE */
"FREE DDN(INFILE)"
EXIT

READIT:
"EXECIO 1 DISKR INFILE"
IF RC <> 0 THEN EOF = "YES"
RETURN
```

Reading one record at a time into the Internal Data Queue – example:
If you have a very large file you won't be able to read it all at once. Your program will terminate with the message "machine storage exhausted".

Here is an explanation of the program, where it is different from the one on the preceding page.
- I find it more convenient to use a subroutine for the reading.
- the number "1" in the EXECIO command makes it read one record at a time
- you can't FINIS until the end
- you need to examine RC after each read: a 2 means end of file
- EXECIO 0 with the FINIS option just closes the file.

Chapter 18: Reading and Writing Files: EXECIO

```
"ALLOC DDN(INFILE) SHR REUSE DSN('userid.TEST.DATA')"
"EXECIO * DISKR  INFILE   (STEM RECD. FINIS)"

  DO I = 1 TO RECD.0
     SAY "RECORD READ WAS " RECD.I
  END

"FREE DDN(INFILE)"
```

Reading whole file with EXECIO into an array – example
If you use Compound Variables (sometimes known as an array) you don't have to worry about what may or may not be in the Internal Data Queue.
In addition, with Compound Variables, you can access each record more than once, in any order.
Explanation of the above program.

- **ALLOC** assigns the file pointer name **INFILE** to the file **ABC.DATA**

- **EXECIO** with the **FINIS** action opens, reads the file and closes it. "*" means "read the whole file".

- **STEM RECD.** tells REXX to read records into variables built upon the name **RECD.** note the period after **RECD.** (May use another name instead of **RECD.**).
    REXX puts the first record into **RECD.1**
    The second record goes into **RECD.2**.
    The third into **RECD.3,** and so on.
    REXX will set **RECD.0** to the number of records read.
    If five records were read, **RECD.0** would equal 5, and **RECD.5** would contain the fifth record.

- **SAY "RECORD READ WAS " RECD.I** displays the record whose number corresponds to the number currently found in the variable I

- **FREE** reverses the action of the **ALLOC**

Chapter 18: Reading and Writing Files: EXECIO

Additional options for Reading

To skip 5 records: I.E. read 5 lines but do not transfer data. (Advance the record pointer by 5 lines)
```
"EXECIO 5 DISKR infile-dd  (SKIP)"
```

Read 1 record starting at the fifth.
```
"EXECIO 1 DISKR infile-dd 5"
```

Read 5 records, putting them into the Internal Data Queue (Stack) in reverse order, before anything else that may be in it.
```
"EXECIO 5 DISKR infile-dd (LIFO)"
```

Chapter 18: Reading and Writing Files: EXECIO

The ALLOCATE command for writing.
If the ALLOCATE command doesn't work, your EXECIO will fail with numerous error messages. Let's look at the ALLOCATE command used with writing.

Three possibilities:
1. The file exists and you want to write over it:
`"ALLOC DDN(ddname) OLD REUSE DSN('file-to-write') "`
There is no difference between this ALLOC and the one used for reading, except for OLD. OLD means exclusive access, so no other job or user can read it while you are using it.

2. You need a file just like another:
`"ALLOC DDN(ddname) NEW REUSE DSN('file-to-write')",`
`"LIKE('file-name-used-as-a-model')"`
The LIKE creates a new file just like another one. Everything is the same except the disk volume and the data contents. If the new file exists already, you should use the ALLOC shown in #1 just above, instead. If you don't know if it exists you may use this REXX code:

```
DSN = "'file-name-to-write'"
IF SYSDSN(DSN) = "OK"
THEN
"ALLOC DDN(ddname) OLD REUSE DSN("DSN")"
ELSE
"ALLOC DDN(ddname) NEW REUSE DSN("DSN")" ,
     "LIKE ('file-name-used-as-a-model')"
```

3. There is no model file. My advice is to allocate the file using TSO ISPF option 3.2 before running the program.

Chapter 18: Reading and Writing Files: EXECIO

Or you can do the full ALLOCATE:
```
"ALLOC DDN(ddname) NEW REUSE DSN('file-to-write')" ,
  "LRECL(record-length) RECFM(F B) SPACE(10 10) TRACKS"
```

It's a good idea to use the logic shown just above, with **SYSDSN**, like this:

```
DSN = "'file-name-to-write'"
IF SYSDSN(DSN) = "OK"
THEN
"ALLOC DDN(ddname) OLD REUSE DSN("DSN")"
ELSE
"ALLOC DDN(ddname) NEW REUSE DSN("DSN")" ,
   "LRECL(record-length) RECFM(F B) SPACE(10 10) TRACKS"
```

Chapter 18: Reading and Writing Files: EXECIO

Writing with EXECIO
You can write:
- the entire file all at once (if it's in the Internal Data Queue or an array)
- one record at a time

You can write from:
- the Internal Data Queue
- Compound Variables (an array)

Here is a generic form of the command for writing: (examples follow)

`"EXECIO how-many DISKW ddname (options)"`

Note these points:
- *how-many* is a number, or a function, that tells how many records to write.
    - you should not use "*" here.
        - `QUEUED()` means "the whole Internal Data Queue"
        - `RECD.0` means "the whole array"
- `DISKW` means that you are writing to a disk file.
- *ddname* is the file pointer name you used in a prior `ALLOCATE`.
- *Options* there are a few options of interest:
    - If all options are omitted, it means that the Internal Data Queue (Stack) will be used.
    - If `STEM` is specified, it means that an array formed with a compound variable will be used.
    - `FINIS` if you wish to close a file at the finish of the read or write operation, you may specify the option `FINIS`.

The Devious '*'.

`"EXECIO * DISKW OUTFILE"`

I've seen an * used in writing. I don't use it, because it requires a null line to signify "end of file".
What if you wanted to write a null line? You wouldn't be able to.
There is never any need to use '*' on an output file.

Chapter 18: Reading and Writing Files: EXECIO

```
"ALLOCATE DDN(OUTFILE) NEW REUSE DSN('userid.TEST2.DATA')",
  " LIKE('userid.TEST.DATA')"

"NEWSTACK"
QUEUE "THIS WILL BE PUT IN THE FILE"
   /*whatever you put on the stack since NEWSTACK
       will be written*/

"EXECIO" QUEUED() "DISKW OUTFILE (FINIS)"

"DELSTACK"
"FREE DDN(OUTFILE)"
```

Writing whole file from the Internal Data Queue – Example:
Here is an explanation of the program:
- **ALLOC** is used to connect your program with the output file. See the preceding pages on **ALLOC**.
- **NEWSTACK** protects the current contents of the Internal Data Queue
- **QUEUE** places something into the Internal Data Queue. In a real program your data would come from a more useful place.
- **EXECIO** uses the **QUEUED()** function (outside of quotes) to specify how many lines are to be written. **FINIS** closes the file. If you don't close the file, you can't **FREE** it.
- **DELSTACK** reverses the action of **NEWSTACK**
- **FREE** reverses the action of the **ALLOC**.

Chapter 18: Reading and Writing Files: EXECIO

```
/* assuming the array is already loaded, and that RECD.0 tells how many
records are in it */

"ALLOCATE DDN(OUTFILE) OLD REUSE DSN('userid.TEMP3.DATA')"

"EXECIO"  RECD.0 " DISKW OUTFILE (STEM RECD. FINIS)"

"FREE DDN(OUTFILE)"
```

Writing whole file with EXECIO from an array – example

Explanation of program:
- be sure **RECD.0** contains the number of records to be written. It is, if you used the array in an **EXECIO DISKR**
- you don't have to use "**RECD.0**" You can use a different name.
- **RECD.0** is used in the **EXECIO** command to specify how many records are to be written. Be sure that it contains a valid number!

Do Practice Problems 64 – 67.

Chapter 19: The INTERPRET Instruction

Chapter 19 is about how you can ask REXX to treat *data* as an instruction.
REXX is an interpreted language. The INTERPRET instruction puts the power of interpretation in your hands. You can create REXX statements or system commands and execute them.

Chapter 19 contains:
    Why INTERPRET?   176

Chapter 19: The INTERPRET Instruction

Why INTERPRET?
REXX is already an interpreted language, so why is there an INTERPRET instruction? Because you may want to build a REXX instruction (REXX can't understand it when it's in pieces) and have REXX process the finished product.

INTERPRET says "OK, REXX, you saw this, but you thought it was only data. Now I'm telling you to have another look – see, it's really a REXX instruction. Execute it."

```
INSTR = "SAY"
VAR   = "HELLO"
INTERPRET INSTR VAR    /*becomes SAY HELLO*/
```

If you didn't have the INTERPRET:

```
INSTR = "SAY"
VAR   = "HELLO"
INSTR VAR
```

REXX would pass the contents of **INSTR** to TSO. It's because (without **INTERPRET**) REXX can't see inside the variable **INSTR** to tell that it contains a REXX instruction, **SAY**.
Not knowing what's there, it happily passes it to TSO.
(TSO rejects it, because **SAY** is not a TSO command).

Chapter 19: The INTERPRET Instruction

Please try this example:
```
SAY "PLEASE ENTER YOUR NAME"
PULL NAME
SAY "THANK YOU, " NAME " NOW ENTER YOUR AGE "

PULL AGE
INTERPRET  NAME "=" AGE
/*if name was JOE, it assigns the variable JOE
   the value of his age*/

SAY "WHOSE AGE DO YOU WANT TO RETRIEVE?. ENTER NAME"
 PULL NAME

INTERPRET "SAY " NAME
/*if name was JOE, it executes the instruction
   SAY JOE*/
```

Do Practice Problem 68.

Chapter 20: Running REXX in Batch, with JCL

Chapter 20 shows you how you can get the full power of REXX in a batch program. You can send your REXX program to batch to execute while you get a coffee.

Chapter 20 contains:
    Example   180

Chapter 20: Running REXX in Batch, with JCL

Example

```
//* valid JCL job statement goes here
//TSOBATCH EXEC PGM=IKJEFT1A,
// DYNAMNBR=200
//SYSEXEC  DD DSN=userid.REXX.EXEC,DISP=SHR
//SYSTSPRT DD SYSOUT=*
//SYSTSIN  DD *
PROFILE PREFIX(userid)
%MYPROG
/*
```

You can run a REXX program in batch. You are executing the TSO Line Mode Interface program, **IKJEFT1A** which calls your program, MYPROG in this example. (Alternatively, execute **IKJEFT01**).

DYNAMNBR=200 allows 200 files to be allocated even if they are not specified in the JCL (dynamic allocation). This is not required in recent versions of the operating system.

This does not make ISPF available, so you can't talk to ISPF.

The **SYSEXEC DD** statement declares your REXX program PDS which contains, in this example, the program **MYPROG**.

Please use the **PROFILE PREFIX** TSO command to specify your TSO user id which is used to check your file and database authorizations. If you don't specify it, the operating system will get your user-id from the security system.

%MYPROG is equivalent to typing **TSO %MYPROG** from the ISPF command line when on-line. The % is optional, but improves execution time.

You may use the optional JCL parameter **PARM='%MYPROG'**, for example
//TSOBATCH EXEC PGM=IKJEFT1A,PARM='%MYPROG' as an alternate way of executing the program instead of what's shown above.

If your program does reads and writes, and needs files, it can use **ALLOC** commands as shown in the chapter on **EXECIO** or (not both at the same time for the same file) it can use ordinary JCL DD statements.
For example, for reading, add this JCL statement to the above:
//INFILE   DD DSN=userid.ABC.DATA,DISP=SHR

Chapter 21: Example Programs, with Explanations

Chapter 21 contains examples of REXX programs, functions, and macros. A REXX program is one that you generally execute from the command line of any ISPF panel or from ISPF option 6. (See Chapter 1.) A REXX function is called or invoked from inside a REXX program. (See Chapter 14.) A REXX macro is executed while you are in an ISPF Editor session. (See Chapter 12.)

Chapter 21 contains:
    STQUICK Program   182
    CANJOB Program   184
    SUBJCL1 Program   186
    SUBJCL2 Program   188
    SUBJCL3 Program   192
    UPDTMEMB Program   196
    CONTAINS Function   200
    EQWILD Function   202
    $HIDEALL Macro   204

All of these examples can be found here:
http://TheAmericanProgrammer.com/programming/rexx2.examples.shtml
Using COPY and PASTE, you can acquire copies of them for your own use.
You will also find them on the CBT Tape, here: http://www.cbttape.org/cbtdowns.htm
Scroll down to File # 911.

Chapter 21: Example Programs, with Explanations

STQUICK, illustrated on the opposite page, is an example of a REXX program that will give you a quick summary of the number of jobs that you have submitted, and their place in the execution queue.

It illustrates the use of **OUTTRAP**, looping, Compound Variables (arrays), and the **POS** function.

[1] It executes the **OUTTRAP** function to capture the displayed output of the TSO command **STATUS**. [2] The output is not displayed on the screen.

Each line of the output of **STATUS** is placed in an element of `"LINE."`. The first line is placed in `LINE.1`, the second in `LINE.2`, etc. After the last line is captured, the line count is placed in `LINE.0`. `"*"` means that all lines are to be captured.

[3] Variables are initialized here.

[4] The first loop checks for the words "NO JOBS FOUND". If that is in the display, the program tells you and exits.

[5] The second loop walks through the lines of the displayed output, and adds to a counter, determined by what is in the display.

These two loops could have been consolidated into one loop, but the program would have become more complicated. I thought it best to separate them rather than have two dissimilar logic structures in the same loop.

Future releases of TSO may display slightly different information, and this program will need to be changed. This is not very likely to happen.

Chapter 21: Example Programs, with Explanations

STQUICK REXX Program. See explanation on the opposite page.

```
/*REXX STQUICK
 COUNT AND STATUS OF JOBS SUBMITTED BY YOU
*/
CALL OUTTRAP "LINE.","*"        [1]
"STATUS"                               [2]
CALL OUTTRAP "OFF"

EXECUTING_CTR = 0       [3]
WAIT_CTR      = 0
OUTPUT_CTR    = 0

DO I = 1 TO LINE.0                     [4]
   IF POS("NO JOBS FOUND",LINE.I) > 0
   THEN
     DO
        SAY "YOU HAVE NO JOBS IN THE SYSTEM NOW"
        EXIT
     END
END I

DO I = 1 TO LINE.0              [5]
   IF POS("EXECUTING",LINE.I) > 0
      THEN EXECUTING_CTR =   EXECUTING_CTR + 1
   IF POS("OUTPUT QUEUE",LINE.I) > 0
      THEN OUTPUT_CTR =         OUTPUT_CTR    + 1
   IF POS("WAITING FOR",LINE.I) > 0
      THEN WAIT_CTR =           WAIT_CTR      + 1
END I

SAY "EXECUTING"              EXECUTING_CTR
SAY "ON OUTPUT QUEUE"        OUTPUT_CTR
SAY "WAITING FOR EXECUTION"  WAIT_CTR
```

Chapter 21: Example Programs, with Explanations

CANJOB, illustrated on the opposite page, is an example of a REXX program that will display the names and JES job numbers of jobs that you have submitted. You may then type in the job suffix and JES job number of a job that you want to cancel. It purges all printed and spooled output of the job as well. Suffix is the letter or number following your user-id, in the job's name.

It illustrates the execution of a TSO command with variables, and terminal dialogue with PULL.

The TSO command ⎡1⎤ **STATUS** looks in the MVS/z/OS batch job execution queue for jobs that you submitted, I.E. with a job name equal to your TSO user-id plus a letter or number suffix. It displays those jobs along with their JES job number.

⎡2⎤ JES refers to the Job Entry Subsystem, a component of MVS/z/OS that manages jobs and their printed or spooled output. This has been tested on a system with JES2.

⎡3⎤ This **PULL** instruction expects you to type in two character strings: the job suffix, and the JES job number. The program then constructs a TSO **CANCEL** command, using your user-id, the job suffix, and the JES job number.
If you just hit ENTER, the program displays a message telling you how to use it, and ends.

⎡4⎤ The **TRACE C** is not required. It displays the complete CANCEL command that is being passed to TSO.

⎡5⎤ I show two ways of concatenating character strings in a TSO command. The first way, the way that is actually executed, uses the concatenation operator, "||" (hex 4F). This joins consecutive character strings, stripping blanks that were between them.
The second way uses consecutive double quotes to concatenate. It works just as well as the first way, but is harder to decipher when first seen. I put this inside of a comment.

An example of a CANCEL command that the program might pass to TSO would be:
CANCEL TSOUSERA(JOB1234), PURGE

Chapter 21: Example Programs, with Explanations

CANJOB REXX Program. See explanation on the opposite page.

```
/* REXX NAME: CANJOB

   PURPOSE: DOES A STATUS, THEN ASKS YOU FOR JOB SUFFIX,
            AND JES JOB NUMBER
            THEN CANCELS THE JOB WITH A PURGE

   USE: %CANJOB
        THEN REPLY WITH JOB SUFFIX,
        I.E. LETTER/NUMBER APPENDED TO YOUR USERID ON JOB NAME
        AND JES JOB NUMBER, NUMERIC PART ONLY

        FOR EXAMPLE:

        %CANJOB
        - MESSAGE APPEARS: TSOU01A(JOB01234) EXECUTING
        A    1234
*/
"STATUS"                                              | 1 |
 SAY "TO CANCEL ONE OF YOUR JOBS,"
 SAY "- TYPE IN:"
 SAY "- JOB SUFFIX     JES JOB NUMBER "                | 2 |
 SAY "- EXAMPLE:       P   1234 "
 SAY
 PULL SUFFIX NUMBER        | 3 |
 IF SUFFIX = ""
 THEN
    DO
       SAY "NEED JOB SUFFIX AND JOB NUMBER, NO COMMAS"
       EXIT
    END
 IF SUFFIX = "" THEN EXIT
 IF SUFFIX = "STOP"   THEN EXIT

TRACE C | 4 |


"CANCEL" USERID() || SUFFIX || "(JOB" || NUMBER"), PURGE"    | 5 |
/* ALTERNATIVELY, YOU COULD HAVE DONE IT THIS WAY:
"CANCEL" USERID()""SUFFIX"(JOB"NUMBER"), PURGE"

The command created will be like this:
CANCEL useridP(JOB1234), PURGE
*/
```

Chapter 21: Example Programs, with Explanations

SUBJCL1, on the opposite page, is an example of a program that will submit JCL to the batch system. It illustrates one technique for creating JCL. It creates a temporary dataset, and then places the lines of the JCL stream into the Internal Data Queue (the Stack).
Then an **EXECIO** is done which reads from the Internal Data Queue, and writes all of the lines in the Queue to the dataset.
A TSO **SUBMIT** command is done.
The temporary dataset is deleted.

You cannot execute this program exactly as it is. You have to change the lower case "userid" to your actual TSO user-id. You also have to modify the first three lines: the JOB statement, to conform to your installation's requirements. Do not remove the `//    TYPRUN=SCAN,` statement. It prevents the fictitious program specified in the JCL from actually executing.

This is a fairly simple program. Nevertheless, many things can go wrong. One in particular that is frustrating is that the temporary dataset may already exist and be in use and open by another program. In that case, the initial **DELETE** will fail and nothing will work. This is not preventable, but it should not happen very often. Doing a lot of error checking for that will lead to a more complex program, and I have not done it.

| 1 | The file name and program name are an example. Use any name you want. |

| 2 | We attempt to delete the temporary file, but it may not exist, so we hide any error messages from the **DELETE** command. |

| 3 | **ALLOCATE** commands can fail for many reasons. We catch that error with an **ERROR** trap. |

| 4 | The **ALLOCATE** command creates and catalogs a dataset. REUSE means that it is OK to use the **DDNAME** even if it is already in use. |

| 5 | Before placing things into the Internal Data Queue, it's a good idea to create a new one, with the **NEWSTACK** TSO command. When finished with the Queue, you should do a **DELSTACK** to delete anything that might be left in the Queue. |

| 6 | **EXECIO** here writes records from the Internal Data Queue, by default, so there is no keyword needed to select the Queue. **FINIS** closes the file. |

| 7 | **FREE** releases the dataset, and disconnects it from the DDNAME that we used. |

| 8 | The temporary file is not needed any longer, so we can delete it. |

| 9 | The actual error trap. |

Chapter 21: Example Programs, with Explanations

SUBJCL1 REXX Program. See explanation on the opposite page.

```
/* REXX SUBJCL1
   SUBMITTING JCL FOR BATCH PROCESSING.
   INSERTING VARIABLE VALUES INTO THE JCL
   USING THE INTERNAL DATA QUEUE

   QUEUE LINES OF JCL, THEN WRITE TO A FILE
   FROM THE DATA QUEUE.
   SUBMIT THE FILE, THEN DELETE IT
*/

TEMP_FILE_NAME = "'userid.TEMP.SUBMIT.CNTL'"           1
PROGRAM_TO_EXECUTE = "MYPROG1"

CALL MSG "OFF"
"DELETE" TEMP_FILE_NAME           2
CALL MSG "ON"

SIGNAL ON ERROR           3
"ALLOC DDN(TEMPFILE) NEW REUSE DSN("TEMP_FILE_NAME")",      4
    "SPACE(3,1) TRACKS"
SIGNAL OFF ERROR

"NEWSTACK"           5
QUEUE "//useridA   JOB (0),'TSO USER',"
QUEUE "//          TYPRUN=SCAN,   "
QUEUE "//          MSGLEVEL=1,CLASS=A,NOTIFY=userid"
QUEUE "//STEP1     EXEC PGM="PROGRAM_TO_EXECUTE
QUEUE "//INFILE    DD DSN=userid.INPUT.FILE,DISP=SHR "
QUEUE "//OUTFILE   DD SYSOUT=A "
QUEUE "//SYSIN     DD * "
QUEUE DATE() TIME()
QUEUE "/*"
           6
"EXECIO" QUEUED() "DISKW TEMPFILE (FINIS)"
"DELSTACK"
"FREE DDNAME(TEMPFILE)"
"SUBMIT" TEMP_FILE_NAME           7
CALL MSG "OFF"
"DELETE" TEMP_FILE_NAME           8
CALL MSG "ON"
EXIT
           9
ERROR:
SAY "UNABLE TO ALLOCATE TEMPORARY FILE" TEMP_FILE_NAME
SAY "TERMINATING"
EXIT
```

187

Chapter 21: Example Programs, with Explanations

SUBJCL2, illustrated on the opposite page, is an example of a program that will submit JCL to the batch system.

It illustrates one technique for creating JCL. It creates a temporary dataset, and then places the lines of the JCL stream into the elements of a compound variable (also called a stem variable, or an array).

<u>1</u> If you load a compound variable and plan to use it in **EXECIO**, you must create elements whose names differ only by the last part, and the last part must be numeric. You are creating consecutively numbered elements, starting with 1, and continuing for as long as you have elements to add. You must also set the zero element to the number of lines that you have loaded.

So, if you load 10 lines into a compound variable named **LINE.**, **LINE.1** will equal the first line, `LINE.10` will equal the last line, and **LINE.0** will equal 10.

When you have a compound variable loaded in this way, you have an array.

This is a fairly simple program. Nevertheless, many things can go wrong. One in particular that is frustrating is that the temporary dataset may already exist and be in use and open by another program. In that case, the initial **DELETE** will fail and nothing will work. This is not preventable, but it should not happen very often. Doing a lot of error checking for that will lead to a more complex program, and I have not done it.

<u>2</u> **call add_line_to_array** invokes a subroutine. It is much more convenient to add a line to the array using a subroutine, than to do it all inline.

<u>3</u> You cannot execute this program exactly as it is. You have to change the lower case "userid" to your actual TSO user-id. You also have to modify the first three lines: the **JOB** statement, to conform to your installation's requirements. Do not remove the **// TYPRUN=SCAN,** statement. It prevents the fictitious program specified in the JCL from actually executing.

Explanation continues on page 190.

Chapter 21: Example Programs, with Explanations

SUBJCL2 REXX Program. See explanation on the opposite page.

```
/* rexx subjcl2
   submitting JCL for batch processing.
   Inserting variable values into the JCL
   using a compound, or stem variable

   place lines of jcl into the stem variable
   write the file,
   submit the file, then delete it
*/
Temp_file_name = "'userid.TEMP.SUBMIT.CNTL'"
Program_to_execute = "MYPROG1"

call msg "off"
"delete" Temp_file_name
call msg "on"

signal on error
"alloc ddn(tempfile) new reuse dsn("Temp_file_name")",
   "space(3,1) tracks"
signal off error

line_counter = 0
call add_line_to_array,
     "//useridA JOB (0),'TSO USER',"
call add_line_to_array,
     "//         TYPRUN=SCAN,   "
call add_line_to_array,
     "//         MSGLEVEL=1,CLASS=A,NOTIFY=userid"
call add_line_to_array,
     "//STEP1    EXEC PGM="PROGRAM_TO_EXECUTE
call add_line_to_array,
     "//INFILE   DD DSN=userid.INPUT.FILE,DISP=SHR "
call add_line_to_array,
     "//OUTFILE  DD SYSOUT=A "
call add_line_to_array,
     "//SYSIN    DD * "
call add_line_to_array,
     DATE() TIME()
call add_line_to_array,
     "/*"
/* display contents of stem variable */
do i = 1 to line.0
   say line.i
end i
```

Program continues on page 191.

Chapter 21: Example Programs, with Explanations

Explanation of **SUBJCL2**, continued.

| 4 | This **EXECIO** statement writes records to the temporary file specified in the **ALLOCATE** earlier in the program.
EXECIO is treated like a TSO command, and therefore needs to be inside of the quotes, except for the variable parts.
LINE.0 is a Compound Variable. It must contain a number. The number is the count of lines that the **EXECIO** will write. **LINE.0** was set earlier in the program.
DISKW is a keyword for **EXECIO**, meaning "write to disk."
TEMPFILE is the **DDNAME** specified in the **ALLOCATE** command earlier in the program. We could have chosen a different name, other than **TEMPFILE**.
STEM is a keyword for **EXECIO**, meaning that **EXECIO** is to get the lines of the records to write from a stem variable.
LINE. is the name of the stem variable that we have set in this program. It doesn't have to be "**LINE.**", it could have been something else.
FINIS is a keyword, meaning "close the file after writing all the records." You must close the file before you **FREE** the file.

| 5 | **FREE DDNAME** is a TSO command. You must break the connection established between the dataset and the **DDNAME** in the **ALLOCATE** command. If you don't do this, it will not be available for use by other programs.

| 6 | **SUBMIT** is a TSO command. It presents a file to the batch processing system which places it in an execution queue.
CALL MSG "OFF" hides any message from the **DELETE** command, or other TSO commands. | 7 |
DELETE gets rid of our temporary file. We no longer need it.
CALL MSG "ON" there is no need to hide messages from TSO commands any longer.

| 8 | **add_line_to_array:** This is a subroutine. It increments a line counter and keeps **LINE.0** set to the current line count.

Chapter 21: Example Programs, with Explanations

REXX program **SUBJCL2**, continued.

<u>4</u>

```
"execio" line.0    "diskw tempfile (stem line. finis)"

"free ddname(tempfile)"    5

"submit" Temp_file_name    6

call msg "off"
"delete" Temp_file_name    7
call msg "on"
exit

error:
say "Unable to allocate temporary file" Temp_file_name
say "terminating"
exit

add_line_to_array:    8
arg line_to_add
line_counter       = line_counter + 1
line.0             = line_counter
line.line_counter  = line_to_add
return
```

Chapter 21: Example Programs, with Explanations

SUBJCL3, illustrated on the opposite page.

This shows how to create and submit JCL using the TSO Line Mode Editor.
CLIST users used this technique a lot. But when REXX appeared, many, including me, tried to use the same technique in a REXX program. I soon discovered that things didn't work the same way in REXX and in CLISTs. In a REXX program, you have to put the Line Mode Editor commands in the Internal Data Queue, or Stack. Then you end your REXX program. The commands that you placed in the Queue are treated as if you had typed them in at the terminal, and are taken as manual input for the Line Mode Editor.

[1] **TRACE C** This is in a comment. I suggest removing the comment delimiters when you are testing this, so that you will see the commands passed to TSO and Line Mode Edit.

[2] Setting the temporary file name: the name chosen doesn't matter, but I suggest including "TEMP" in the name, so you know it's not something that you will need later.

[3] I put the JCL delimiter "/*" in a variable. That way it's less likely to be mistaken for a REXX comment delimiter.

[4] We are deleting the temporary file. It should contain nothing of importance. If it doesn't exist, the **DELETE** command will give an unpleasant error message, which we have hidden by means of the **CALL MSG "OFF"**.

[5] Creating a new, temporary file with **ALLOCATE**. This command creates a file with a record length of 80, a blocksize of 8000, and a fixed blocked record format. This is MVS/z/OS terminology, knowledge of which is a prerequisite for creating JCL and submitting jobs, and writing REXX programs on TSO.

Explanation continues on page 194.

Chapter 21: Example Programs, with Explanations

SUBJCL3 REXX Program. See explanation on the opposite page.

```
/* REXX SUBJCL3
   SUBMITTING JCL FOR BATCH PROCESSING.
   INSERTING VARIABLE VALUES INTO THE JCL.
   USING THE TSO LINE MODE EDITOR TO CREATE
   A TEMPORARY FILE, SUBMIT IT,
   AND EXIT WITHOUT SAVING IT
*/
/* TRACE C  */          1
TEMP_FILE_NAME = "'userid.TEMP.SUBMIT.CNTL'"      2
PROGRAM_TO_EXECUTE = "MYPROG1"
JCL_DELIMITER = "/*"         3

/* DELETE, IF IT EXISTS. IT'S A TEMP FILE.

   YOU SHOULD HAVE NOTHING GOOD IN A TEMP FILE. GOODBYE.
*/
CALL MSG "OFF"           4
"DELETE" TEMP_FILE_NAME
CALL MSG "ON"

"ALLOCATE DSN("TEMP_FILE_NAME") NEW REUSE TRACKS",         5
   "SPACE(3,1) LRECL(80) RECFM(F,B) BLKSIZE(8000)"
```

Program continues on page 195.

Chapter 21: Example Programs, with Explanations

Explanation of **SUBJCL3**, continued.

| 6 | First we **QUEUE** the lines of the JCL that we are creating. What we put in the REXX Internal Data Queue will be seen by the Line Mode EDIT command, later. You have to do it this way, before you execute the EDIT command. The EDIT command will look for lines of input from the user. However, by placing the lines in the Queue, we are fooling EDIT into thinking that we are typing the lines in.

| 7 | Then we **QUEUE** a null line to tell Line Mode EDIT that it should not look for additional lines of input, but instead to look for commands that it understands. (We could have done a **QUEUE** with nothing else on the line, for the same result.) **LIST, SUBMIT and END NOSAVE are EDIT** commands.

| 8 | **LIST** displays the lines that it has inserted into the file.
SUBMIT sends the file to the batch system to be run as a background job. | 9 |
END NOSAVE exits from **EDIT** without saving the file. | 10 |

| 11 | The **EDIT** command is near the end of the program. It starts up the Line Mode Editor, which immediately looks for input from the user. (You will see its message line "**INPUT**").
CNTL means that the file contains JCL.
OLD means that the file exists.
NONUM means that the file doesn't contain line numbers.

You cannot execute this program exactly as it is. You have to change the lower case "userid" to your actual TSO user-id. You also have to modify the first three lines: the JOB statement, to conform to your installation's requirements. Do not remove the **// TYPRUN=SCAN,** statement. It prevents the fictitious program specified in the JCL from actually executing.

| 12 | **STATUS** is not needed, but will come in handy while you are testing. It is the TSO command which interrogates the batch system about all jobs whose names are equal to your TSO user-id plus a character.

If you don't queue Line Mode Editor commands correctly you will find yourself IN the Line Mode Editor, manually, and not in your REXX program, and temporarily not in ISPF. To get yourself out, type in **"END NOSAVE"**. You may have to hit ENTER first.
Test thoroughly, so that you don't leave an unsuspecting user in a program that he or she is unfamiliar with.

This method works, but I don't recommend it. I include it because you see it in some programs that were converted from CLISTs.

This technique is simple: but check the syntax and order of the commands carefully. If you don't invoke the Line Mode Editor properly, the commands will be passed to TSO for execution. Sometimes that produces an error and does no damage; sometimes the commands cause TSO to try to execute them, with unpredictable results.

Chapter 21: Example Programs, with Explanations

REXX program **SUBJCL3**, continued.

```
QUEUE "//useridA JOB (0),'TSO USER',"    6
QUEUE "//          TYPRUN=SCAN,   "
QUEUE "//          MSGLEVEL=1,CLASS=A,NOTIFY=USERID"
QUEUE "//STEP1    EXEC PGM="PROGRAM_TO_EXECUTE
QUEUE "//INFILE   DD DSN=USERID.INPUT.FILE,DISP=SHR "
QUEUE "//OUTFILE  DD SYSOUT=A "
QUEUE "//SYSIN    DD * "
QUEUE DATE() TIME()
QUEUE JCL_DELIMITER
QUEUE "" /* NULL LINE EXITS INPUT MODE */    7
QUEUE "TOP"
QUEUE "LIST"              8
QUEUE "SUBMIT"        9        10
QUEUE "END NOSAVE"
"EDIT" TEMP_FILE_NAME "CNTL OLD NONUM"       11
"STATUS"    12
```

Chapter 21: Example Programs, with Explanations

UPDTMEMB, illustrated on the opposite page, is a REXX program that will obtain information about a PDS (Partitioned Data Set, or library), and create or update a member in the PDS named ##INFO with that information. The program was written as an illustration. It does not do anything useful.
It illustrates the use of ARG, the REXX function **LISTDSI, OUTTRAP, EXECIO** from a stem variable, and terminal dialogue using **PULL**.

[1] **ARG PDS .** This picks up the first word (character string delimited by spaces) that you type on the command line if you execute the program by specifying just its member name. For example, if you type **UPDTMEMB MY.PDS.DATA** the **ARG** statement picks up **MY.PDS.DATA** and places it in the variable **PDS**. The dot, or period, on this statement discards a second word and any word entered after that.

[2] **LISTDSI(PDS)** invokes the REXX function **LISTDSI**. This function interrogates TSO about the PDS. It returns information about the PDS in a set of reserved variables, for example **SYSDSORG**, **[3]** which contains the Data Set Organization. In the case of a PDS, **SYSDSORG** will be **"PO"**. In the case of a sequential (flat) file, it will be **"PS"**.

[4] **SYSDSNAME** contains the fully-qualified name of the PDS (with no apostrophes). Why did we do this? We already had the name of the PDS. The reason is that my program is written so as to allow you to type in the PDS name in one of two ways:
– a fully-qualified name, including your user-id or other high-level qualifier, bounded by apostrophes (').
– an unqualified name, minus your user-id, without apostrophes.
It is much easier to construct a PDS name + member name if you have the fully-qualified name. And that is what we did in the line:
PDS_AND_MEMB = "'"SYSDSNAME"("##INFO")'"

[5] We do an **OUTTRAP**, asking it to capture all the lines that **LISTDS** will display, in the stem variable LINE.

[6] **"LISTDS" PDS** executes the TSO command **LISTDS**. Normally this command displays dataset or PDS attributes at the terminal. However, we have prevented that by doing an **OUTTRAP**.

[7] **CALL OUTTRAP "OFF"** allows TSO commands to display their output at the terminal, as they normally do.

Explanation continues on page 198.

Chapter 21: Example Programs, with Explanations

UPDTMEMB REXX Program. See explanation on the opposite page.

```
/* REXX UPDTMEMB
   OBTAIN MEMBER INFORMATION ABOUT A PDS,
   UPDATE A MEMBER IN THAT PDS NAMED ##INFO
   WITH THAT INFORMATION.
   1 PARAMETER REQUIRED TO BE ENTERED ON THE COMMAND LINE:
   PDS
   IF IT IS NOT ENTERED ON THE COMMAND LINE,
   THE PROGRAM WILL ASK FOR IT.
*/

ARG PDS .                          ▢1
DEBUG = "NO"                               /* YES OR NO */

IF PDS = "" THEN CALL GET_INPUT    /* NO ARG, ASK FOR INFO */

/* INITIALIZE VARIABLES */
MEMBER_NAME = "##INFO"

/* VERIFY PDS */
RET_CODE = LISTDSI(PDS)            ▢2
IF RET_CODE <> 0 THEN SIGNAL BAD_DSN

IF SYSDSORG <> "PO" THEN SIGNAL NOT_PDS    ▢3

/* BUILD FULL DSN + MEMBER NAME
   LISTDSI RETURNS THE FULL NAME OF THE PDS
   IN THE RESERVED VARIABLE SYSDSNAME
*/
PDS_AND_MEMB = "'"SYSDSNAME"(##INFO)'"      ▢4
IF DEBUG = "YES" THEN SAY "FULL NAME IS " PDS_AND_MEMB

/* CAPTURE OUTPUT OF LISTDS */
CALL OUTTRAP "LINE.","*"           ▢5
                        ▢6
"LISTDS" PDS
                            ▢7
CALL OUTTRAP "OFF"
IF DEBUG = "YES" THEN CALL DISPLAY_LINE_ARRAY
```

Program continues on page 199.

Chapter 21: Example Programs, with Explanations

Explanation of **UPDTMEMB**, continued.

<u>8</u> Before writing to a file, a valid **ALLOCATE** command must be done, to link the existing PDS to a symbolic name, or **DDNAME** (file handle) of our choice. We have chosen "**OUT**"
We are using **SHR**. **SHR** allows other users or jobs to allocate the PDS as long as they also use SHR.
The member name does not have to exist. If it exists, it will be overwritten. If it doesn't exist, it will be created.

<u>9</u> This **EXECIO** statement writes records to the PDS specified in the **ALLOCATE** earlier in the program.
EXECIO is treated like a TSO command, and therefore needs to be in quotes, except for the variable parts.
LINE.0 is a stem variable. It must contain a number. The number is the count of lines that the **EXECIO** will write. **LINE.0** was set earlier in the program.
DISKW is a keyword for **EXECIO**, meaning "write to disk."
OUT is the **DDNAME** specified in the **ALLOCATE** command earlier in the program.
STEM is a keyword for **EXECIO**, meaning that **EXECIO** is to get the lines of the records to write from a stem variable.
LINE. is the name of the stem variable that we have set in this program. It doesn't have to be "**LINE.**", it could have been something else.
FINIS is a keyword, meaning "close the file after writing all the records." You must close the file before you **FREE** the file.

<u>10</u> **FREE DDNAME** is a TSO command. You must break the connection established between the dataset and the **DDNAME** in the **ALLOCATE** command. If you don't **FREE** a file, it will not be available for use by other programs.

Chapter 21: Example Programs, with Explanations

REXX program **UPDTMEMB**, continued.

```
WRITE_TO_FILE:
IF DEBUG = "YES" THEN TRACE C
"ALLOCATE DDNAME(OUT) DSNAME("PDS_AND_MEMB") SHR REUSE"       8
IF DEBUG = "YES" THEN SAY "GOING TO WRITE " LINE.0 " RECORDS"

"EXECIO " LINE.0 "DISKW OUT (STEM LINE. FINIS)"       9
IF RC = 0 | RC = 1 THEN SAY "MEMBER CREATED SUCCESSFULLY"
ELSE SAY "MEMBER CREATION FAILED"
IF DEBUG = "YES" THEN SAY "RETURN CODE FROM EXECIO " RC
"FREE     DDNAME(OUT)"       10
RETURN

GET_INPUT:
   SAY "ENTER THE NAME OF A PDS, STANDARD TSO NAMING CONVENTIONS"
   SAY "INFORMATION ABOUT THE PDS WILL BE COLLECTED"
   SAY "AND INSERTED INTO THE PDS IN MEMBER NAME ##STATS"
   PULL PDS
   IF PDS  = "" THEN DO
      SAY "NOTHING ENTERED, ENDING"
      EXIT
      END /* NO PDS   SECOND TIME */

RETURN

DISPLAY_LINE_ARRAY:
DO I = 1 TO LINE.0
   SAY "TRAPPED LISTD" I LINE.I
END I
RETURN

BAD_DSN:
SAY "DATASET NAME ENTERED DOES NOT EXIST" PDS
EXIT

NOT_PDS:
SAY "DATASET NAME ENTERED IS NOT A PDS" PDS
EXIT
```

Chapter 21: Example Programs, with Explanations

CONTAINS function, illustrated on the opposite page.

This illustrates an internal function, the use of the REXX built-in function **ARG()**, and the **RETURN** statement.

It may also be used as an external function, and would then be accessible by other REXX programs as well. If you make it external, its name must begin with a letter, contains letters and numbers, and be up to 8 characters in length, since it will be a member on a PDS or library, and that is the requirement for names of PDS's. If you use it as an external function, delete the instruction: **CONTAINS: PROCEDURE**

[1] A function gets its input through the **ARGs**.
This function uses the built-in function **ARG()** to pick up the first and the second argument string passed to it. **ARG(1)** gives the first argument string, and **ARG(2)** gives the second. The argument strings must be separated by a comma.

[2] A function must end with a **RETURN**, and the **RETURN** must pass some information back.
The information may be a number or a character string, or the null string (" ").

There is nothing magic about returning a 1 or a 0. Some built-in REXX functions return a 1 when the results are positive, some return a 0. We have chosen a 1. There is no convention about returning a -1 for an error.

An alternate way of picking up the argument strings would have been as follows:
ARG string1, string2
Then the function would look like this, in its entirety:
```
/* REXX CONTAINS*/
ARG string1, string2
if string1= "" | string2 = "" then return -1   /* 2 args required */
if pos(string1, string2)  > 0   then return 1
return 0
```

Chapter 21: Example Programs, with Explanations

CONTAINS function. See explanation on the opposite page.

```
/* REXX CONTAINS
A REXX internal function that tells you if the first argument
is contained in the second.

If you wish to use it as an external function
     you need to delete the instruction:
CONTAINS: PROCEDURE

It is executed this way, as an example: (in another program!)
Haystack = "Hello!"
Needle = "!"
If contains(needle,haystack) = 1 then say "OK"
else say "Must contain exclamation (!) character"

say contains("cat","reallocate") gives 1
say contains("cat","kate")       gives 0
say contains("cat")              gives -1
*/
CONTAINS: PROCEDURE
```
⬜ 1
```
if arg()              < 2 then return -1   /* 2 args required */
if pos(arg(1),arg(2)) > 0 then return 1
return 0
```
⬜ 2

Chapter 21: Example Programs, with Explanations

EQWILD function, illustrated on the opposite page. This is an example of an internal function.

There are many ways of doing comparisons in REXX, but none of them allow the use of wild card characters. This function lets you use a wild card character in the comparison.

It illustrates the use of the **PARSE SOURCE** REXX instruction, the **ARG** instruction, the **STRIP** function and the **SUBSTR** function.

[1] This statement protects variables, and is a good idea for internal functions:
EQWILD: PROCEDURE
You have to delete that statement if this becomes an external function.

[2] The initial **ARG** instruction picks up 2 or three strings passed to it. The strings are separated by commas. The **ARG** instruction uses a period in the final position. This deletes any fourth or subsequent string passed to it.

[3] The **STRIP** function with the **"B"** operand drops leading and trailing blanks in the strings.

[4] Both strings must be of the same length.

[5] This loop walks through the input strings, character by character. If it finds a mismatch, except for a wild character, it returns a 0, indicating a non-match.
If it completes the loop with no mismatches, it returns a 1, indicating equality.

[6] This is one way to find out if the function was executed erroneously as a program. **PARSE SOURCE** returns several items of information. The second item can be **COMMAND**, if this was executed as a program; **SUBROUTINE** if this was executed by REXX **CALL**; **FUNCTION** if this was invoked as a function, like this: **FUNCTIONNAME(arguments)**.

To understand what a "program" is: it's REXX code that is *not* called by a REXX **CALL**, or by a function invocation. It's sometimes called a main program.

Chapter 21: Example Programs, with Explanations

EQWILD function. See explanation on the opposite page.

```
/* REXX EQWILD
This is an internal function that does a comparison,
with a wild card character.
The wild card character is always equal to
the corresponding character in the input strings.
Comparison is done character by character.
Both strings must be of the same length.
The default wild character is the underscore: (_).
It is used like this: (in another program!)
if eqwild("JO_N", "JOAN", "_")
     then say "equal"
     else say "not equal"
The first input string may contain the wild card character.
*/
EQWILD: PROCEDURE       1
arg string1, string2, char1_wild .     2
call validate
if char1_wild = "" then char1_wild = "_"

string1 = strip(string1,b) /* drop lead + trail blanks */   3
string2 = strip(string2,b)

if length(string1) <> length(string2) then return 0    4

do i = 1 to length(string1)     5
   if substr(string1,i,1) = char1_wild then nop
   else if substr(string1,i,1) <> substr(string2,i,1)
   then do
           return 0 /* not equal*/
        end
end i
return 1 /* equal */

validate:
parse source . how_called .      6
if how_called = "COMMAND" then do
   say 'this is a function'
   say 'it may not be called from the command line'
   say 'call it from another REXX program:'
   say '   if eqwild("JO_N", "JOAN", "_")'
   say '       then say "equal"'
   say '       else say "not equal"'
   exit -1 /* give -1 to TSO,
           since program was called from command line */
   end
return /* was called properly */
```

Chapter 21: Example Programs, with Explanations

HIDEALL macro. illustrated on the opposite page.

This is a macro that you can execute within a TSO/ISPF Editor session. It excludes, or hides, all lines in the file being edited that contain a specific character string.
This is the opposite of these two Editor commands commonly done in sequence:
EXCLUDE ALL
FIND ALL character-string

It must be a member in the same PDS as your main program, or in a PDS allocated to **SYSEXEC**, or specified in an **ALTLIB** command. The name doesn't have to start with a "$".

[1] You must start your macro with **ADDRESS ISREDIT**. It must be done before you try to send any commands to the Editor.

[2] **"MACRO (PARM1)"** is how you pick up arguments passed to the macro on the command line. Note this is not at all the same as picking up arguments with **ARG** or **ARG()**. The two methods are incompatible with each other. **"MACRO (PARM1)"** works only with macros, while **ARG** or **ARG()** work only with REXX main programs, functions or subroutines.

[3] I checked the return code in RC after the **"MACRO (PARM1)"** instruction. A non-zero return code tells me that the program was executed with the word **"TSO"** in front of it, on the command line of any TSO/ISPF screen, or that it was executed outside of the TSO/ISPF Editor. The program must be ended. I could have put a -1 on the **EXIT** instruction, to tell TSO that there was an error. Instead, I displayed a message.

[4] Three commands are passed to the TSO/ISPF Editor. The user could have typed these three commands on the command line to obtain the same result as from this macro.

I could have done one **ADDRESS ISREDIT** on a separate line, followed by **"EXCLUDE ALL"** and the two other ISPF Editor subcommands. There would have been a savings of a few fractions of microseconds of CPU time.

Chapter 21: Example Programs, with Explanations

HIDEALL macro. See explanation on the opposite page.

```
/* REXX $hideall
A macro for the TSO/ISPF editor.
Used within a TSO/ISPF edit session.
It excludes (hides) all lines of the file which
contain a specific character string.

To use, within a TSO/ISPF edit session,
type $HIDEALL character-string on the command line.
Example:
$HIDEALL DSN=
*/
ADDRESS ISREDIT                    [1]
"MACRO (PARM1)"            [2]

IF RC > 0 THEN SIGNAL NOT_AS_A_MACRO    [3]
IF PARM1 = "" THEN EXIT
ADDRESS ISREDIT "EXCLUDE ALL"              [4]
ADDRESS ISREDIT "FIND ALL '"PARM1"'"
ADDRESS ISREDIT "FLIP "
EXIT /* NORMAL END OF PROGRAM */

NOT_AS_A_MACRO:
SAY "THIS IS A TSO/ISPF EDITOR MACRO"
SAY "IT MAY BE EXECUTED ONLY IN THE ISPF EDITOR"
SAY "BY TYPING $HIDEALL char-string ON THE COMMAND LINE"
EXIT
```

Index

!, 91, 93
!C, 93
!I, 94
!R, 94
%, 13, 22, 113
&&, 50
&, 50
&LASTCC, 36
**, 113
-, 92
*, 113, 171
*/, 14, 24
-, 113
/*, 14, 24
/, 113
//, 113
:, 16
;, 15
?I, 91, 94
?R, 91, 94
¬=, 46
_, 27
|, 50
||, 35
+, 113
+++, 92
<, 46
<<, 47
<=, 46
<>, 46
=, 45, 46
==, 45, 47
>, 46
>.>, 92
><, 46
>=, 46
>>, 47
>>=, 47
>>>, 92
>C>, 92
>F>, 92
>L>, 92
>O>, 92
>P>, 92
>V>, 92
¬<, 46
¬<<, 47
¬==, 47
¬>, 46
¬>>, 47
Abutting strings, 35
Accept input from terminal, 33
Action of PARSE, 68
ACTIVATE, see ALTLIB
Addition, see Math
ADDRESS ISPEXEC, 122, 123
ADDRESS ISREDIT, 120, 124, 125, 204
ADDRESS TSO, 121

ALLOCATE, 162, 163, 169, see also EXECIO
ALTLIB, 20, 144, 145
AND with IF, 50
Apostrophes around commands, 15, 116, 117
Apostrophes with literals, 30, 31
ARG, 65, 68 - 72, 141
Arithmetic, see Math
Array, see Compound Variables
ASCII, 132
Assign a file, see ALLOCATE
Assigning variables, 14, 15, 26, 128 - 129
ATTN, 22, 56, 91, 96, 97, 104
Bar, vertical, 35, 50
Batch execution of REXX, 13, 121, 180
Boolean operators, 50
Built-in Functions, 128-138
C2D, 133
C2X, 133
CALL 16, 38, 97 – 102, 129
CALL ON ERROR, 100, 101
CALL ON SYNTAX (no such thing)
CALL OUTTRAP, 136, 159, 182
CALLing a function, 129
Cancel program, see Interrupt program
CANCEL, TSO command, 184
CAPS ON, 20
Case in comparisons, 44
CASE Structure, 60, 61
Case, 14, 15
Change name of trap, 98
Close a file, 165 - 167
Codes displayed during Interactive Debug, 92
Colon, 16, 32
Column delimiting with PARSE, 86, 87
Column rules, 14
Comma, 16, 70, 71, 72, 128, 129, 141, 144
Command line and PARSE, see ARG, PARSE ARG
Commands, 9, 37, 116, 126
Commas and ARG, 69, 70, 141
Comment, initial, 14, 24
Comparison operators, 45 – 47
Comparisons, case, 44
Compound Variables, 27, 54, 156-160, 173, 188
Concatenating data strings, 35
Concatenation operator, 35
CONDITION("D"), 105
Conditional, 41-50
Continuing literals, 30
Convert to uppercase, see Uppercasing
Create a member, 19, 20
Create library/PDS, 18
D2C, 133
D2X(ABS(RC)), 105
D2X, 133
Data Queue, see Internal Data Queue
Data Set List, 21
Data Strings, concatenating, 35
Datatype declarations, 14

DATATYPE, 130
DDNAME, 78, 162-164, 170, 171
DEACTIVATE, see ALTLIB
Deallocate a file, see FREE
Debugging, 89-94
DELSTACK, 151 – 153, 165, 172
DIGITS, NUMERIC, 114
DISKR, 164, 168, 173
DISKW, 131, 150, 171 - 173
Display on the Terminal, 25
Display source program, 90, 105
Division, 113
DO ... END, 34, 48, 49, 52, 53
DO FOREVER, 56, 57
DO UNTIL, 55
DO WHILE, 55
Double quotes around commands, 15, 116, 117
Double quotes around name of function or subroutine, 145
DROP, 29
DSN, 163, 169, 170, 180
E /(setup), 19
EBCDIC, 132, 133
Editor profile, 20
ELSE, see IF
END IF, (no such thing) see DO
End subroutine or function, 16, 28
End the program, 16, 36, 56
Ending a function or subroutine, 16, 28
Environment commands, see Commands
Equal, 45
ERROR trap, 96, 100
ERRORTEXT(RC), 105
Exclusive OR, 50
EXECIO, 162-173
Execute program through JCL, 180
Execute program, 13, 21
EXECUTIL TS, 91
EXIT, 16, 36, 56
Exponentiation, 113
EXPOSE, 143
Extension, compound variable, 157
EXTERNAL, 65, 74
External, user-written functions, 144, 145
FAILURE trap, 96, 102
FIFO, 39, 150, 164
File pointer, 162, 163
Files, reading and writing, see EXECIO
Find a character string in another, 130
FINIS, 165
FOREVER, DO, 56, 57
FORMAT, 130
FREE, 162, 165, 166, 167, 172, 173
Function, Internal, 140 – 145, 200 - 202
Functions, built-in, 128 – 138
Functions, writing your own, 72, 140 – 145
GO TO, (no such thing) see SIGNAL
Greater than or equal to, 46
Greater than, 46

Halt Interpretation, 91, 104
HALT trap, 91, 96, 104
HEX, 132
HI, 91, 104
HILITE LOGIC, 20
HILITE REXX, 20
IF, 41 – 50
IKJEFT01, 121, 180
IKJEFT1A, 121, 180
Initial Comment, 14, 24
Input from the terminal, 33
Integer divide, 113
Interactive Debug, 90, 91
Intermediate results, 94
Internal Data Queue, 65, 73, 74, 149 – 153
Internal Function, 140 – 145, 200 – 202
INTERPRET, 176, 177
Interrupt program, 22, 56, 91, 96, 97, 104
ISPEXEC, 120, 122
ISPF Editor, commands for, see ISREDIT
ISPF Member List, 13
ISPF Option 3.2, 18
ISPF, commands for, 122 – 124
ISREDIT, 120, 124, 125, 204
ITERATE, 52, 58
JCL Delimiter, 192
JCL, run REXX through, 180
Label, 16, 32
LEAVE, 52, 56, 57
Leftovers, 153
LENGTH, 130
Less than or equal to, 46
Less than, 46
Library member list, 21
Library, see PDS
LIFO, 39, 150, 168
LIKE, 169
Line Mode Editor, 192, 193
Line number, see SIGL
LISTCAT, 37
LISTDSI, 134, 196
Literal and PARSE, 66, 83
Literal, 15, 30
Looping, 51 – 58
MACRO, 124, 125, 204
Main program and ARG, 69 – 71
Math operators, 113
Math, 25, 26, 112 – 114
Member, create, 19, 20
MSG, 135
Multiplication, 113
NAME in SIGNAL or CALL, 98
Naming variables, 27
Nesting of IF, 44, 49
NEW in ALLOCATE, 170
NEWSTACK, 151, 153, 165, 172, 187
NOP, 44
Not equal, 45, 46
Not greater than, 46
Not less than, 46

NOVALUE trap, 96, 103
Null string, 68
NULLS ON ALL, 20
NUMBER OFF, 20
Numbers with PARSE, 86, 87
NUMERIC DIGITS, 114
Numeric test, 130
OLD, 169, 170, 173
Operators, arithmetic, 113
Operators, Boolean, 50
Option 3.2, 18
OR with IF, 50
OTHERWISE, 39, 60, 61
OUTTRAP, 136, 159, 182
Overview of REXX, 12 – 16
PA1, 22, 56, 91, 97, 97, 104
Parenthesis in arithmetic, 113
PARSE action, 68
PARSE ARG, 65, 69 – 72
PARSE columns, 86, 87
PARSE EXTERNAL, 65, 74, 151
PARSE Origins, 65, 66
PARSE PULL, 65, 73, 151
PARSE SOURCE, 66, 77
PARSE Templates, 80 – 87
PARSE VALUE, 66, 76
PARSE VAR, 66, 75
PARSE VERSION, 67, 79
PARSE with numbers, 86, 87
PARSE, 64 – 87
PARSE, basic form, 64
PARSE, short forms, 68
Passing commands to TSO, 37
PDS member list, 21
PDS, create, 18, 19
Percent Sign, 13, 22, 113
Period in Compound Variables, 156, 157
Period to absorb data, 81
Pointer, file, 162, 163
POS, 130
Practice problems, web page, 10, 25
Precision in arithmetic, 114
PROCEDURE, 143, 144
PROFILE PREFIX, 180
PROFILE, Editor, 20
Program, end, 16, 36, 56
Protecting variables, 143, 144
PULL, 33, 73, 151
PUSH, 39, 73, 131, 150
QSTACK, 152, 153
QUEUED(), 131, 152, 153, 172, 187
Quotes around commands, 15, 116, 117
Quotes around name of function or subroutine, 145
Quotes with literals, 30
RC, 28, 105, 116, 118, 119, 152, 162
RECD.0, 167, 171, 173, 188, 189
Remainder, 113
Reserved variables, 28
RESULT, 28, 129, 142, 144
Return Code, see RC

RETURN, 16, 28, 140 – 144
REUSE, 163, 165, 166, 167, 169, 170, 172, 173
REXX in Batch, 180
REXX overview, 12
REXX with JCL, 180
SAY, 25
Search Order for Functions and Subroutines, 145
SELECT, 60, 61
Semicolon, 15
SEND, 31, 37
Setting Up, 18 – 22
Short forms of PARSE, 68
SHR, 163, 165, 166, 167, 180,
SIGL, 28, 99, 100, 102 – 105
SIGNAL OFF ERROR, 100
SIGNAL OFF FAILURE, 96, 102
SIGNAL OFF HALT, 104
SIGNAL OFF NOVALUE, 103
SIGNAL OFF SYNTAX, 99
SIGNAL ON ERROR, 100
SIGNAL ON FAILURE, 102
SIGNAL ON HALT, 104
SIGNAL ON NOVALUE, 103
SIGNAL ON SYNTAX, 99
SIGNAL, 32, 56, 97, 108
SKIP, 168
Source program, 90, 105
SOURCE, PARSE, 77
SOURCELINE function, 90, 99, 105
Stack, see Internal Data Queue
STATUS, 184
Stem variables, see Compound variables
STEM, 136, 157, 169, 167
Store variable, 123
Strictly equal, 45, 47
Strictly greater than or equal to, 45, 47
Strictly greater than, 45, 47
Strictly less than or equal to, 45, 47
Strictly not equal, 45, 47
Strictly not greater than, 45, 47
Strictly not less than, 45, 47
Strings, abutting, 35
STRIP, 202
SUBCOM, 126
SUBMIT, TSO command, 186
Subroutine, 32, 148
Subscripted variables, see Compound variables
SUBSTR, 131
Subtraction, 113
SYNTAX trap, 99
SYSDSN, 137, 170
SYSDSNAME, 196
SYSEXEC, 144, 145, 180
SYSPROC, 144, 145
Templates for PARSE, 80 – 87
Terminal and PARSE, 33, 65
Terminal dialogue, 151
Terminal input, 33, 65
Terminal, display on, 25
THEN, see IF

TRACE !, 91, 93
TRACE !C, 93
TRACE !I, 94
TRACE ?I, 91, 94
TRACE ?R, 91, 94
TRACE A, 93
TRACE C, 93
TRACE E, 93
TRACE F, 93
TRACE L, 93
TRACE N, 93
TRACE O, 93
TRACE R, 94
TRANSLATE, 131
Trap contents, 105
Trap name, changing, 98
Trap, change name of, 98
Trapping Unexpected Conditions, 96 – 106
TS, 91
TSO Functions, 134 – 137
TSO ISPF Option 3.2, 18
TSO, commands for, 9, 37, 116 , 120 – 126
Undefine a variable, 29
Undefined variable, 27
Underscore, 27

UNTIL, DO, 55
UPPER, see PARSE
Uppercasing, 64, 69, 73, 87, 131
User-written function, see Functions, writing your own
VALUE, 66, 76
VAR, 66, 75
Variable and PARSE, 66, 75, 85
Variable, assigning, 14, 15, 26
Variable, compound, 27, 54, 156 – 160
Variable, numeric, 14
Variables, 26 – 29
Variables, naming, 27
Variables, protecting, 143
Variables, reserved, 28
Verbs, 38
VERSION, 67, 79
Vertical bar, 35, 50
VGET, 123
VPUT, 123
Web page for setting up, 10, 22
WHEN, 60
WHILE, DO, 55
X2C, 133
X2D, 133

CPSIA information can be obtained
at www.ICGtesting.com
Printed in the USA
LVHW060430300620
659354LV00018B/1829